The Lutheran Church✠Missouri Synod

A Week in the Life of

The Lutheran Church ✝ Missouri Synod

Compiled and edited by the staffs of The Lutheran Church—Missouri Synod Board for Communication Services and Concordia Publishing House.

Thanks to Aid Association for Lutherans, the fraternal benefit society based in Appleton, Wis., for helping to fund production of this book.

To the people of The Lutheran Church—
Missouri Synod. These men, women and children
form the congregations that have joined
together into this church body. Together,
they worship, learn, live and serve in the name
of Jesus Christ.

Their service is dedicated to the ultimate end:
To God be the glory!

A good photograph tells a story. Few things evoke emotion and imagination so powerfully as a photograph. What makes the photographs in this book even more powerful is that they tell a story of *faith*—a faith that's intertwined in the day-to-day business of life.

This book is dedicated to you, the members of The Lutheran Church—Missouri Synod. You, the members who lived the moments captured in these photographs. And to the photographers, some professionals and some amateurs, who strived to capture those representative moments with their talents, time and gift of human vision.

AAL is honored for the opportunity to support the creation of this book, *A Week in the Life of The Lutheran Church—Missouri Synod.*

John Gilbert

John Gilbert
President and Chief Operating Officer
Aid Association for Lutherans

A Week in the Life of The Lutheran Church—Missouri Synod

Christ's people in their congregations are the very heart of a church

IN Alaska, a congregation uses a tiny trailer for its office. Another, in Texas, renovates a multibuilding complex, fully intending to use every bit of space in what was once the world's largest auto mall. In Hawaii, members in bright print clothing worship outdoors; in Wisconsin, they don their "Sunday best" to worship in the 156-year-old brick and stone building built by their great-grandparents.

"Sent Forth by God's Blessing"

Whether they gather in small, white-frame churches next to century-old cemeteries or in new, soaring, glass-and-steel worship centers, they share a common confession centered in the Gospel—the Good News: "For God so loved the world that He gave His one and only Son, that whoever believes in Him shall not perish but have eternal life" (John 3:16). With 2.6 million others, these are the people who form a church body called The Lutheran Church—Missouri Synod.

There is no better way to explain an organization than to *show* it at work. That's the purpose of this book: to give an up-close look at the people and the congregations of The Lutheran Church—Missouri Synod. You'll see them as people from the congregation next door or from the congregations across town, in other states and around the world.

You'll find these people in church on Sunday, the traditional day of worship, but you'll also find them in many places during the other six days of the week—in Christian vocations where their faith directs and sustains them. You'll also find them in faith-motivated activities—studying their Bibles, practicing with the choir, helping the homeless, volunteering at school, making quilts, building a new church or in mealtime prayer.

This is a book about The Lutheran Church—Missouri Synod in its 150th year. It's a series of snapshots, if you please, documenting the week of April 21–27, 1996.

A celebration of congregations

As the Synod celebrates 150 years, it celebrates congregations, the "front line" of the church's ministry.

It is in the congregation that Christ gathers His people around God's Holy Word—to hear it proclaimed, to study it, to proclaim it in worship. In the congregation, through the water and Word of Holy Baptism, God claims each child—young or old—as His own, calling them by name and bringing them into His kingdom. In Holy Communion, Christ is truly and essentially present under the bread and wine, given to His people to eat and to drink, for the forgiveness of their sins, for life and for salvation.

The congregation is the place for confirmations and weddings and funerals—happy and sad transitions in our lives. More than a church building, it is where believers are gathered by Christ through His Word and Sacraments—teaching, caring, laughing, learning, growing, serving.

United for a purpose

Little did they know what they started!

On April 26, 1847, 12 pastors representing 14 congregations signed a constitution that established "The German Evangelical Lutheran Synod of Missouri, Ohio and Other States."  Meeting in Chicago, they had traveled by horseback, stagecoach and boat from Illinois, Indiana, Iowa, Michigan, Missouri, Ohio and New York. (Also attending were 10 advisory pastors, four laymen, two theology candidates and seven guests.)

They were men of faith and conviction. Some were German immigrants who had come to the United States to preserve their Lutheran confession of the faith, free from government intervention. They were stirred for mission, especially to reach German immigrants, and, for some, the desire to bring the Gospel to Native Americans.

In its 150th year, The Lutheran Church—Missouri Synod (the name was shortened on the 100th anniversary) counts 2.6 million members in 6,175 congregations. The original constitution was  written in German (and German continued to prevail in worship and writing until World War I). Today, the list of pastors includes names like Schmidt and Nguyen and Perez and O'Connor and Zyskowski and King and Pacilli. While English dominates now, on any given Sunday, there may be worship in at least 20 different languages—including Spanish, Hmong, Eritrean, Russian, Finnish, Slovak, Chinese, even German.

Walking together

"Synod" comes from the Greek words that mean "walking together." It has rich meaning in this church body, because the congregations voluntarily choose to belong to the Synod. Diverse in their service, these congregations hold to a shared confession of Jesus Christ as taught in Holy Scripture and the Lutheran Confessions.

With the universal Christian Church, The Lutheran Church—Missouri Synod teaches and responds to the love of the Triune God: the Father, Creator of all that exists; Jesus Christ, the Son, who became  human to suffer and die for the sins of all human beings and to rise to life again in the ultimate victory over death and Satan; and the Holy Spirit, who creates faith through God's Word and Sacraments. The three persons of the Trinity are coequal and coeternal, one God.

Being "Lutheran," the congregations accept and teach Bible-based teachings of Martin Luther that inspired the reformation of the Christian Church in the 16th century. The teaching of Luther and the reformers can be summarized in three short phrases: Grace alone, Scripture alone, Faith alone.

• Grace alone—God loves the people of the world, even though they are sinful, rebel against Him and do not deserve His love. He sent Jesus, His Son, to love the unlovable and save the ungodly.

• Scripture alone—The Bible is God's

inerrant and infallible Word, in which He reveals His Law and His Gospel of salvation in Jesus Christ. It is the sole rule and norm for Christian doctrine.

• Faith alone—By His suffering and death as the substitute for all people of all time, Jesus purchased and won forgiveness and eternal life for them. Those who hear this Good News and believe it have the eternal life that it offers. God creates faith in Christ and gives people forgiveness through Him.

The congregations of the Synod are "confessional." They hold to the Lutheran Confessions as the correct interpretation and presentation of Biblical doctrine. Contained in *The Book of Concord: The Confessions of the Evangelical Lutheran Church*, these statements of belief were put into writing by church leaders during the 16th century.

The Synod is advisory in regard to congregations. Through circuits (groups of eight to 10 congregations), districts (35 in the United States) and national conventions, they elect officials and determine policies and directions for the church body. Congregations call their own pastors and determine local activities, subject to their bond to abide by the Scriptures and the Lutheran Confessions.

In broad terms, The Lutheran Church—Missouri Synod serves to support congregations and act in their behalf. The support includes services and resources to help them be effective in their local ministries. In behalf of congregations, the Synod operates colleges and seminaries; conducts international mission programs; and provides health, disability and retirement benefits for church workers. Congregations and individuals also support social services, world relief, disaster response and radio and television programs.

Tradition and vision

The Lutheran Church—Missouri Synod celebrates its anniversary with a vision that reflects strong tradition, yet points to the future. Proposed by current President A. L. Barry and adopted by the Synod in convention, the vision is of a church body that is:

• Strong in the Word—all we do is rooted in the Holy Scriptures as a means to grow in faith and in understanding God's love in Jesus Christ.

• Christ-centered and people-sensitive—with Christ as our Lord and Savior, caring for people marks the disciple of Jesus Christ, attending to the physical needs of people as well as the spiritual needs of those who are lost without faith.

• Boldly reaching out with the Gospel—sharing that Jesus Christ died for sinful human beings, rose again and offers to everyone free forgiveness and eternal life.

• Faithful to the Scriptures and the Lutheran Confessions—holding that the Scriptures are the infallible and inerrant standard for doctrine. The Lutheran Confessions are a true exposition of Scripture and a pure declaration of the truth of God's Word.

• Marked by peace and unity—trusting that believers can settle differences in a peaceful manner under the banner of God's own love and forgiveness, united by Scripture and the Lutheran Confessions.

The making of 'A Week in the Life . . .'

This is a book prepared by the people of The Lutheran Church—Missouri Synod. Hundreds of men and women volunteered countless hours, talents, creativity and expense to share the work of their congregations and members.

"A Week in the Life . . ." was conceived in the summer of 1995 by staff members from the Synod's Board for Communication Services and Aid Association for Lutherans, the fraternal benefit society based in Appleton, Wis. AAL helped to fund the production of the book on behalf of its 1.7 million members as a gift to the Synod in celebration of its 150th Anniversary.

A planning team met in September 1995, recommending that the project cover a full week; that it emphasize the lives of congregations and their members; that it focus on people; and that the "week" be April 21–27, 1996 (the first week in the Synod's 150th year).

The book became a joint project of the Board for Communication Services and the Synod's Concordia Publishing House (CPH). Ambitious plans called for it to be completed by October 1996—start-to-finish in less than six months. (Normally, a book of this size requires a year for production.)

In late December, 1995, a mailing invited congregations to suggest photo ideas and to encourage applications from photographers. Almost 500 congregations  responded, and they or the photographers were contacted by telephone to discuss the project. In March, 1996, the photographers were sent forms for photo releases, a waiver of photo rights, forms for caption information and an "advance payment"—a coupon for two rolls of film!

The "shooting" was done during April 21–27, and by early May Communication Services began receiving boxes and packages—eventually exceeding 8,000 pictures! While the 450 photographers were asked to submit their 10 best, many sent their 20 best, even entire folders of slides and pictures.

Some photographers also called to say their congregation enjoyed the project and had decided to produce their own "week in the life" books and displays. Many photographers took vacation days (some, a full week) to concentrate on the project.

Communication Services staff provided coordination and a system to track photographers and photographs. Staff wrote copy and captions and made an initial  "edit" of the photos. CPH staff designed the book, laid out the pages, assisted in writing captions and arranged printing, distribution and marketing. To bring the book to completion in record time, CPH staff used the latest in computer publishing technology. Final decisions on design and selection were shared by the staffs.

To say the selection was difficult is to play with understatement. A book twice this size may have been easier! Photos were selected on the basis of quality, reflection of diverse ministries and activities, geographic representation and inclusion of as many photographers as possible.

The following pages make a book by and about us—to celebrate together and to share this "family photo album" with the rest of the world.

The Lutheran Church—Missouri Synod
Board for Communication Services
Rev. Paul Devantier
Project Director

I rejoiced with those who said to me, "Let us go to the house of the Lord" (Ps. 122:1).

A farmer spreads cocoa beans to dry in the sun. His village is one of the locations where missionaries aid The Lutheran Church of Nigeria, a partner church. In Nigeria, as in many countries where the Synod has missionaries, the emphasis is on training lay preachers who bring the Gospel to their fellow countrymen. *(Barbara Ross)*

A new life in the day of Jenna Kelsey Minges—Baptism! Family members line up to take pictures at Pinnacle, Rochester, N.Y. From left, sponsors Deborah and William Susie, Pastor Delbert Tiemann (holding Jenna) and parents Christopher and Mary Minges. *(Roger Williams)*

Previous page:
Members gather for worship at St. Paul, Fairmont, Minn., on April 21. On this Sunday, more than one million people worshiped in the 6,175 congregations of The Lutheran Church—Missouri Synod. *(Roger Carlson)*

Worship at First Trinity, Tonawanda, N.Y., begins soon, but first the candles must be lighted. Acolyte Katie Poling gets help from usher Walter Zimberg. *(David Young)*

Members of Ascension, Littleton, Colo., opened their week in Palestine, by building friendships with a sister congregation. Saliba A. Faddoul, left, principal of Bethlehem Lutheran Christmas Church, meets with Bob Wagner, Ascension's stewardship chairman. *(Arnold Voigt)*

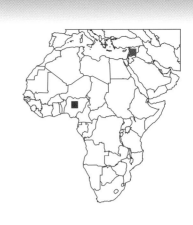

Near Hebron on the West Bank in Palestine, a group from Ascension and Our Father, both congregations in Littleton, Colo., visit a shepherd's cave. The Colorado Lutherans were visiting a sister congregation in Palestine. *(Arnold Voigt)*

Amal Nasser, right, explains the history of a Palestinian vineyard near Hebron to American visitors from Ascension, Littleton, Colo. Listening, from left, are Gerald Albrecht, Annette Wolfer, David Oppenheim and Judy Voigt. *(Arnold Voigt)*

Spring flowers add a royal appearance in front of the Lutheran Church of the Cross, Hanover, Mass. *(Anton Materna)*

13

At a mission festival in Schenectady, N.Y., members of Zion learn more about Lutheran Hour Ministries' Orphan Grain Train. From left: Christine Bauer, Susan Haswell and speaker Elfriede Eberle. *(Herb Hanke)*

Jim Possinger serves as the radio announcer, introducing the broadcast of the worship from St. John in Depew, N.Y. *(Marsha Barber)*

Missouri Synod missionaries and their families gather for a "family picture" at Miango Rest Home in Nigeria. *(Barbara Ross)*

Elder Paul Potucek, arranges Communion cards after worship at St. John in Hazelton, Pa. Later, he will record names in the congregation's Communion attendance book. On the wall is a flag bearing stars—one for every member who served in World War II. (*Lil Junas*)

Surrounded by God's creation, students from Baltimore Lutheran High School take a break on the Gunpowder River near Hereford, Md. They are attending a weekend spiritual growth retreat. (*Martha Bainbridge*)

Bible study offers an occasion for smiles and conversation at the student center of All Saints in Slippery Rock, Pa. The ministry emphasizes outreach to international students. From left are Fanny Mahoney, Carolyn Denise Pratt, Augusta R. Mennell (campus ministry director) and Shirley Wong. (*Augusta R. Mennell*)

Confirmation student Ton Pham robes for his acolyte responsibilities at Martin Luther Chapel, Pennsauken, N.J. Originally from South Vietnam, he has lived in the United States for five years. (*Kenneth Wunsch*)

No sun, but lots of Son! It's 6:45 a.m. and participants at the Gulf States District Convention of the Lutheran Women's Missionary League gather for a sunrise service at Gulf Shores, Ala. Rev. Scott Stewart, district LWML counselor and pastor of St. Paul, Picayune, Miss., leads the worship. *(Bea Daily)*

Karol Selle of Ann Arbor, Mich., speaks to the Gulf States District Convention of the Lutheran Women's Missionary League. As director of public relations, she brings greetings on behalf of the president of the International Lutheran Women's Missionary League. *(Bea Daily)*

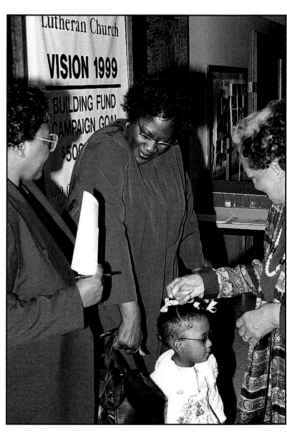

Enjoying fellowship after worship at Prince of Peace, Charlotte, N.C., are, from left, Verlene Glover, Betty Morris, little Deidra Kilgo and her aunt, Carol Kilgo. *(Clarence T. Nolley Jr.)*

Speaking to a joint meeting of youth from Resurrection (LCMS) and Our Savior (a congregation of the Evangelical Lutheran Church in America) in Cary, N.C., Rep. Fred Heineman tells how God influences his life and his work in the U.S. Congress. Heineman is a member of St. Philip (ELCA) in Raleigh, N.C. *(Tom Swanson)*

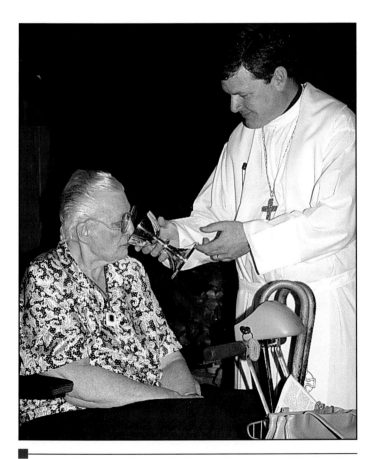

Shed for you. . . . At Concordia, Sarasota, Fla., Edna McKeehan receives Communion from Pastor Edward DeWitt. *(Brenda Flegler)*

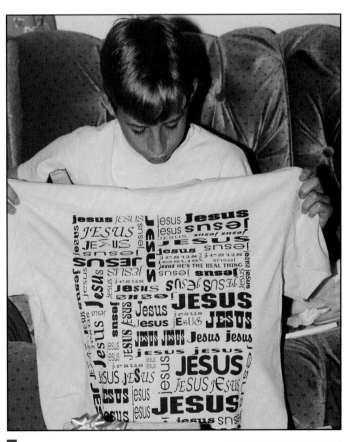

There's no mistaking this message! Raymond Kirklin shows a T-shirt during the celebration for confirmands at Faith, Merritt Island, Fla. The afternoon party is hosted by Pastor Russell Frahm and his wife, Karen. *(Linda Lawrence)*

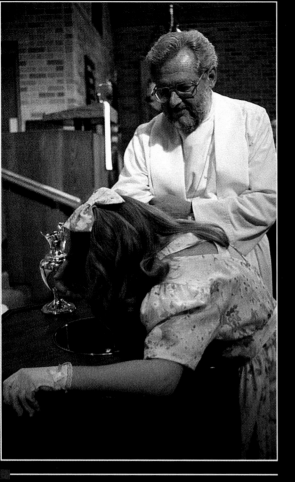

In the name of the Father, Son and Holy Spirit—Brittany Bartholomew is baptized by Pastor David Albertin at Immanuel, Michigan City, Ind. *(John M. Niemann)*

A confimand receives his blessing from Pastor Jon W. Reusch at Cross of Christ, Bloomfield Hills, Mich. *(James L. Fearing)*

Deb Schumm holds up the lesson about Elijah, and Andy Berning provides the answers in Sunday school at Zion, Barrett, Ind. *(Julie Faulkner)*

The youngest and the oldest—member ages span from 10 days to 93 years and both attend worship at Hope, Grand Rapids, Mich. The youngest: little Elon Schantz; the oldest: William James Parker. *(Doug Humphries)*

The men's chorus offers its anthem of praise at Trinity, Jackson, Mich. *(Connie Blackwood)*

Volunteer Bob Leichti makes tapes of the worship at Trinity, Jackson, Mich. Later, members of the congregation will deliver copies to shut-in members. *(Connie Blackwood)*

Worship begins at St. Paul, Millington, Mich. *(Tina Petzold)*

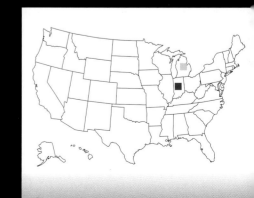

A media ministry cameraman follows the worship at St. Lorenz in Frankenmuth, Mich. The congregation airs its worship three times a week over cable television— once live and twice by video recordings. *(Dale Ahlschwede)*

After the Supper—Roy and Onalee Beck wash and dry Communion cups at Community of Hope, Brecksville, Ohio. *(Deborah Phillips)*

Sound the trumpet! Musicians practice before the worship at St. Mark, Chesterland, Ohio. *(Mark Rychel)*

Surrounded by some of her family is 99-year-old Emma Rabe. They gather in the narthex at St. John, Pinconning, Mich., before the 10:30 service. She has three children, 10 grandchildren, 18 great-grandchildren and nine great-great-grand-children. *(Ron Wetters)*

Sunday school children perform "The Lord Said to Noah" at St. Paul, Ashland, Ky. *(Mary H. Robinson)*

Pastor Peter Ave-Lallemant is greeted with children's hugs at Christ, East Point, Ga. *(Wendy Morris)*

Pastor Karl Davies greets members after the 11 a.m. worship at Trinity, Hammond, Ind. *(John Hassel)*

21

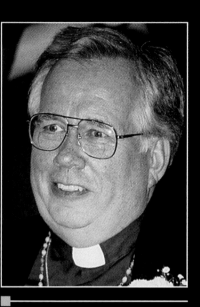

Rev. Ron Bergen, new president of the Ohio District. (*Christine McCune*)

Choir members say good-bye to Rev. Ron Bergen on his last day as pastor. He is leaving Faith Lutheran Church, Kent, Ohio, to assume duties as full-time president of the Ohio District. He succeeds Rev. David Buegler, who left the presidency to take a call to a parish. (*Christine McCune*)

The smiles would be sweet, even without doughnuts. Heidi Ahlersmeyer and Jessica Lehenbauer enjoy having their picture taken before Sunday school at King of Kings, Mason, Ohio. (*Su Polzin*)

Women at Trinity, Athens, Ga., conduct a "Mary Kay" fundraiser for the Lutheran Women's Missionary League. Looking at samples are Chris Geiszler and Jan Harmon. (*Philip Weinrich*)

The large dove overhead provides a reminder that the Holy Spirit is at work where people gather around the Word of God. In this "junior church service" at Zion, Akron, Ohio, are, from left, Stevie Friend, Gabriel Raicevich, Davey Bauer, Christian George and Geoffrey Parker. *(Christine McCune)*

Boarding their motor home, Dale and Lucy Busse, members of Zion, Akron, Ohio, embark on a trip to a Laborers For Christ project. As volunteers, they will help with the construction of a Missouri Synod church building at Beautiful Savior in Fargo, N.D. Many Laborers live in their motor homes or campers while "on the job," which can last several months. *(Christine McCune)*

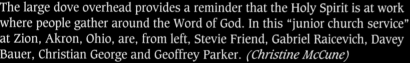

In the balcony, the bell choir waits between songs during worship at Immanuel, Cleveland, Ohio. *(Herman R. Wensel)*

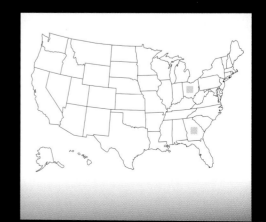

At St. Paul, Chicago Heights, Ill., Anita Wanek, left, learns of God's love in one-on-one confirmation instruction from Doris Bauer. *(Gene Brackman)*

Not quite a cast of thousands, but 135 youngsters from kindergarten to sixth grade fill the front of Faith, Appleton, Wis., for a production of "Go, Go, Jonah." The children's musical provides spontaneous joy to the morning worship. *(Glenn Ocock)*

Smiles and enthusiasm make the music come alive as the children's choir performs at Faith, Appleton, Wis. *(Bob Mickelson)*

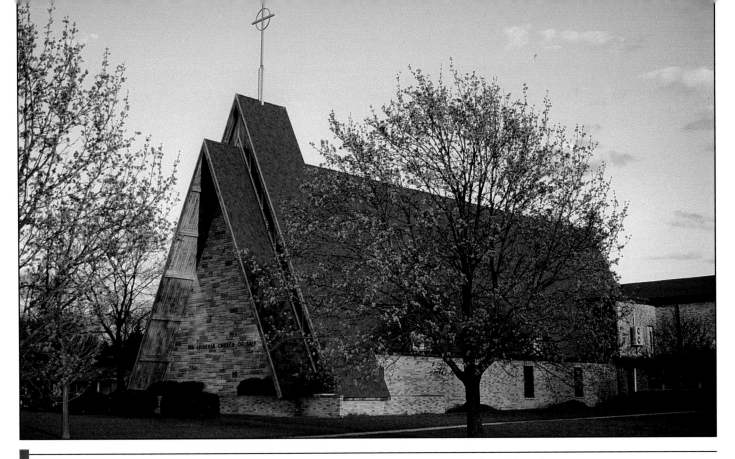

Blue skies and budding trees give a perfect springtime backdrop for St. Luke, Itasca, Ill. *(Rick Nelsen)*

Sometimes, pastors are grandparents too. Little Caleb Ellenbecker stirs admiration from his grandfather, Rev. Gary Paul, pastor of Trinity, Athens, Wis. *(Bob and Sue Heckendorf)*

Members of Trinity, Athens, Wis., dedicate their new school building. Pastor Gary Paul offers thanks as Building Chairman Gary Belanger, Principal Bill Steltenpohl and Congregation Chairman Harvey Zubke hold items for a time capsule. *(Bob and Sue Heckendorf)*

We worship in all forms of structures, including this little log church in northern Wisconsin. This is Our Savior, Bundy/Jeffries, Wis. *(Kurt H. Krahn)*

Working from the balcony, a crew videotapes services at Trinity, Roselle, Ill. The services are shown on local cable TV twice a week. From left are Greg Kettler, Brian Gasteiner and Jeff Jung. *(Greg Kettler)*

No sleeping here! Pastor Roger Pollack delivers a lively sermon during the 9:30 a.m. service at Good Shepherd, Elgin, Ill. *(David Tonge)*

Pastor Robert D. Koeppen greets lifelong member Henry Mahler and his wife, Meta, following morning worship at Zion, Hinsdale, Ill. *(Ruta Jensen)*

American Sign Language gives visual beauty to prayer. Heidi Mueller interprets the Lord's Prayer during worship at Prince of Peace, Palatine, Ill. *(Barbara Arnold)*

Over the altar of St. Paul, Skokie, Ill., is a figure of the risen Christ. *(John Schalk)*

The Lord calls you by name, Lamontrell, Keandra and Alexandria. At Trinity, Memphis, Tenn., Pastor Ronald Wiese baptizes three children. In the photo, from left in the foreground, are Demetrio Beverly, Keandra Beverly, Alexandria Pinkins and Pastor Wiese. Standing are aunt Donna Reed (holding Lamontrell Beverly), great-grandmother Beulah Montgomery and grandmother Jeanie Reed. *(Ronald Wiese)*

Confirmation day—and Ann Westphal, left, gets a big hug from her mother, Pam. They are members of St. Paul, Bonduel, Wis. *(Curt Schneider)*

Organist Don Vogler introduces a hymn at St. Paul, Stevens Point, Wis. *(Randy Lindemann)*

The Easter message is just as meaningful two weeks after Easter Sunday. Adult and youth choirs present "He's Alive! A Celebration of the Living Lord," at St. Luke, Itasca, Ill. *(Rick Nelsen)*

Joyce Marquard, foreground, and Lois Gribble wash communionware after the 10:45 a.m. service at St. Paul, Stevens Point, Wis. *(Randy Lindemann)*

Worship concludes at Immanuel, Freeport, Ill.
(Lynn Hoefle)

Jim Smart comes to the Communion table in his electric wheelchair, along with his wife, Shirley, at St. Paul, Oconomowoc, Wis. Pastor Ron Krug serves the bread and wine. *(Tom Truebenbach)*

On the job at Kickapoo Park in Lincoln, Ill., Ranger Donald Hellman inspects pine trees for insect damage. He is a member of Zion, Lincoln. *(Marlin W. Roos)*

Nursery, kindergarten and first- and second-grade students gather around Arlene Rush for the Sunday school opening at Ascension, East Peoria, Ill. *(Al Knack)*

Youth at Trinity, Pekin, Ill., give their counselor, Jacque Davis, a lift during an afternoon meeting. *(Jim Deverman)*

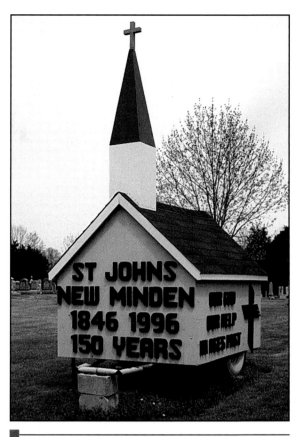

Keith and Jill Schuette exit St. John, New Minden, Ill., after their 2 p.m. wedding. *(Dawn T. Mueller)*

St. John, New Minden, Ill., uses this float in local parades. The congregation, a charter member of the Synod, dedicated its first church building in 1863. *(Ray Hausler)*

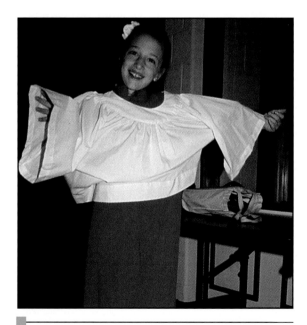

Angelic-looking Mari Montroy dons her surplice and prepares to sing in the children's choir at Holy Redeemer, Dryden, Mich. *(Robert Barker)*

David Stertz and Michael William Henry Stertz, 2, look at a tractor that was owned by Michael's great-grandfather. The father and son are beginning a spring walk, a family tradition for 80 years, spanning six generations. Every member of the Stertz family has been active at Immanuel, Auroraville, Wis. The farm is across the road from the church. *(Nelma Stertz)*

He works on Sunday

Faithful pastors tend to the spiritual lives of their congregation. While Sunday is a busy day, it is often the result of a busy week that includes study and preparation of a sermon and arrangements for the worship—plus calls on members, meetings and administrative responsibilities.

Photographer Scott Strazzante followed his pastor, Rev. Steven Teske, on Sunday morning. These are a few scenes from Pastor Teske's morning at Bethlehem, Chicago, Ill.

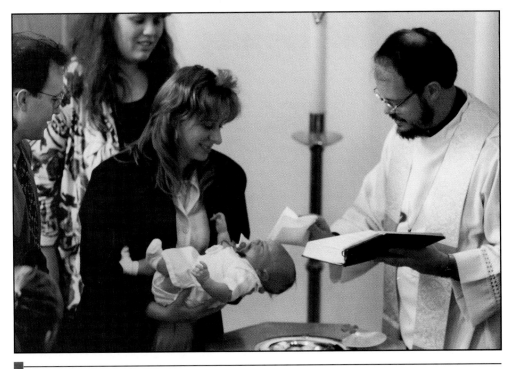

The morning worship includes the baptism of Martin Eagan IV, being held by sponsor Patricia Eagan of Sauk Village, Ill.

Giving a few last-minute thoughts to his sermon, he puts on his crucifix before the worship service.

Holding son Christian, 2, he greets members after the service.

Blessing the congregation near the end of the worship at Bethlehem, Chicago, Ill.

After the service, he and his wife, Robin, hold the hand of twin daughter Magdalena, 4, as her sister, Anastasia, runs by. Robin is expecting her second set of twins.

A chancel drama is presented by the youth group at St. Martin, Winona, Minn. From left are Jennifer Wolfgram, Sarah Stark and Angela Haase. *(Colleen McGuire-Klemme)*

The church bell still calls members to worship at St. Paul, New Melle, Mo., one of the 14 congregations that constituted The Lutheran Church—Missouri Synod in 1847. Alvin Auping rings the bell. *(Barbara Auping)*

Video monitors at Concordia, Kirkwood, Mo., help people in the back pews and overflow areas follow the worship service. The entire congregation is able to see Pastor Vernon Gunderman introduce the child he is baptizing. *(Dan Gill)*

It's been a labor of love and beauty. For nearly 50 years, Marie Drevlow has arranged flowers for the altar at St. John (Green Meadow), Ada, Minn. *(Howard Neumann)*

During the children's sermon at First, Hot Springs, Ark., Clifford Coleman hands out wooden crosses he made. Giving the sermon is Pastor Jonathan Beyer. *(Roy A. Jacob)*

The fellowship hour at Christ Memorial, Affton, Mo., offers opportunity for Megan Glass to share information about Girl Scouts (and maybe sell a few boxes of cookies). *(Al Mueller)*

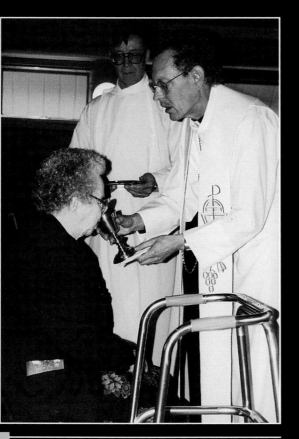

"I just want to be a sheep"—Children join Pastor Terry Grzybowski in song during the children's message at the morning service at St. Paul, Perham, Minn. The message emphasizes the Christian's desire to follow Jesus, the Good Shepherd. *(Cleone Stewart)*

Ethel Esala receives Communion from assistant Ray Niemi and Pastor Dan Clemons at Gloria Dei, Virginia, Minn. *(Annette Herring)*

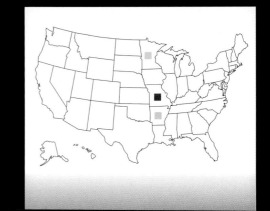

Billy Sylvester and Dan Schewe manage the soundboard for the worship service at Shepherd of the Grove, Maple Grove, Minn. *(John T. Roles)*

Pastor David Marth gets a hug from Carolyn Young. The congregation— Trinity, St. Louis, Mo.—is one of the original congregations to form the Synod. *(King Schoenfeld)*

Youngsters get their chance to participate in groundbreaking for a new building to house Holy Cross in St. Cloud, Minn. *(Lynn Harff)*

Jacob and his 12 sons pose for a family portrait after presentation of the "Joseph" musical at St. Matthew, Columbia Heights, Minn. Men of the congregation and the children's choir presented the show. (*Dick Beyersdorfer*)

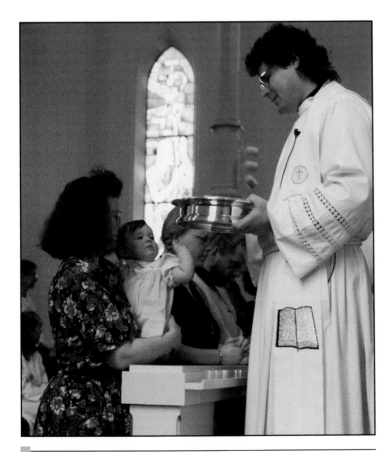

Head usher William Hilbrands arrives early to post the hymns for worship at St. Paul, Perham, Minn. (*Cleone Stewart*)

Lorna Fratzke and her daughter, Lindsey, receive a Communion blessing from Pastor Eric Klemme. The worship is at St. Martin, Winona, Minn. (*Colleen McGuire-Klemme*)

Preserved by the Perry County Lutheran Historical Society, Altenburg, Mo., the Concordia log college/seminary in Trinity Lutheran Church Park is a reminder of the Synod's history. Founded by Saxon immigrants in 1839, it was the first Lutheran seminary west of the Mississippi River and operated until 1849 when the program was transferred to St. Louis. *(Vernon Meyer)*

At their farm in State Center, Iowa, Gilbert and Betsy Berrey try a new water tunnel system for growing tomatoes and herbs. The garden is a project for their congregation, St. John. *(Bonnie Berrey)*

Todd Stocker holds his sleeping son, Nathan, as Pastor David Marth makes announcements at the close of worship at Trinity, St. Louis, Mo. Todd, a second-year student at Concordia Seminary, St. Louis, is a field worker at the church, helping with worship and other duties. On Tuesday, he, his wife, Kellie, Nathan and daughter, McKenzie, will learn of his assignment to a year-long vicarage in Woodbury, Minn. *(King Schoenfeld)*

Karen Ahal, member of St. John, Ellisville, Mo., sets the table for the Lord's Supper before the worship service begins. *(Dave Kuenzel)*

Dana Meyer sings a solo during the service at Christ Memorial, St. Louis, Mo. *(Al Mueller)*

Dave and Tami Peterson and daughter, Morgan, receive information about Shepherd of the Grove, Maple Grove, Minn. Pam Kruger serves as the host at the Welcome Center. *(John T. Roles)*

Three-year-old Rachel helps with farm chores by bottle feeding "Sam" on her family's farm near Waverly, Iowa. Her family belongs to St. Paul, Artesian. *(Kathleen Scott)*

Marie Biesenthal is congratulated by Rev. Walter Tietjen, California–Nevada–Hawaii District president, on the day she receives the Aquila Award from Concordia Publishing House, St. Louis, Mo. The award honors Marie for her leadership and service to the church, including service with the Lutheran Women's Missionary League and as an author and coordinator of study materials. *(Paul Ockrassa)*

Each Sunday morning, the 8 a.m. worship service at St. Paul, Perham, Minn., is taped by volunteers like Jim Jaroszewski. Approximately two dozen tapes are delivered after the service to the Memorial Home and to shut-in members. *(Cleone Stewart)*

In celebration of their 50th wedding anniversary, Ray and Ethel Syrjanen renew their wedding vows. They are members of Gloria Dei, Virginia, Minn. *(Annette Herring)*

Mud is also a wondrous part of God's creation. At 11 months, John Scott celebrates the good gifts! He is the son of Mike and Kathleen Scott, members of St. Paul, Artesian, Waverly, Iowa. *(Kathleen Scott)*

Congregation president Charles Galloway reads the Scripture lessons during worship at Hope, Omaha, Neb. *(Bob Samuels)*

The "Ministering Puppeteers" teach a Gospel lesson for children's church at Shepherd of the Grove, Maple Grove, Minn. The alter egos for the characters on stage are Brandon Lyles, Angela Sylvester, Kelly Gilbert, Julie Kirk, Aislinn Anderson, Brian Anderson, Joel Casey, Tabitha Davey and Mike Warinak. *(John T. Roles)*

At St. Andrew, Wichita, Kan., young people from across the city gather for a worship service hosted by the congregation's youth group. Tiffany Lauffer, left, leads the prayer. In the foreground are Amber Witte and Mike Grauerholz. *(Kathryn Coit)*

At Grace, Arlington, Texas, Robert Spence operates the camera to produce a live broadcast of its worship for a local cable channel. *(Edward Naumann)*

Raising their voices in praise of the mighty God are members of the senior choir at Our Redeemer, Sioux Falls, S.D. Among the singers are Bonnie Jerke and Deb Neumeister. *(Lynda Strobel)*

Taking her turn in the nursery, Katie Schroeder rocks Jonathan Walther during the worship service at St. John, Okarche, Okla. *(Delinda Barnett)*

Elzie Griffin and little Amanda Leigh Roensch talk about Jesus in the nursery during morning services at Concordia, Houston, Texas. *(Ken Garrick)*

The steeple of St. Paul, Ute, Iowa, reaches for the springtime sky. *(Richard N. Thies)*

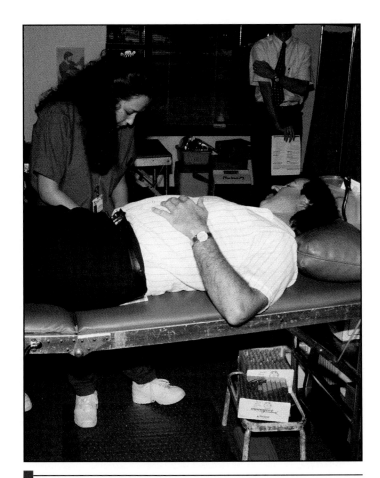

Confirmand Kendra Brack gets some primping from Shannon Pogue, her friend and mentor in Christian growth. They are members of St. Andrew, Wichita, Kans. *(Kathryn Coit)*

Members of Good Shepherd, Duncan, Okla., provide a life-saving community service by sponsoring a blood drive. Darrel Rippee gives his donation with the help of Tina Johnson. *(Roger F. Rensvold)*

43

Offering a different view of worship services: here's a sermon ready to be preached—from the pastor's viewpoint at Fishers of Men, Sugar Land, Texas. *(Thomas N. Van Duzer)*

A seven-piece brass ensemble accompanies worship at Immanuel, Cleveland, Ohio. *(Herman R. Wensel)*

In Neligh, Neb., Darrel and Marlene Timm lead their family in giving thanks to God before their noontime meal. The children, from left, are Nathan, Kendra and Brandon. *(Jennell J. Suhr)*

Steven Smith and Zachary Hunter work on a project during Sunday school at Grace, Kileen, Texas. *(Tim Matthys)*

The "He is Risen!" cross gives a dramatic Easter proclamation to Kansas City, Kan. It stands next to St. Luke in the inner-city community. *(Judith McGuire)*

Pastoral assistant Walter Schramm listens to comments during adult Bible class at Grace, Kileen, Texas. *(Tim Matthys)*

Under the direction of Pastor James Baneck, the choir adds music to a special afternoon worship service at Messiah, Mandan, N.D. The service celebrates the congregation's 40th anniversary. *(Richard Ames)*

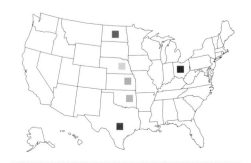

It was an opportunity no fourth-grade Sunday school class could ignore: First a smiling picture from the children of Redeemer, Austin, Texas. . .

. . . Then a chance to be creative! So they add a second pose with their "best" faces! Laughter too is a gift from God to be shared in the church. *(Art Aubry)*

On their way to worship at Trinity, Grand Island, Neb., are Irma and Vic Bosselman. At ages 88 and 90, they have been Missouri Synod members all their lives. *(LaVerne Fuller)*

Although his wife, Doris, says he "fishes eight days a week," Dale R. Clark also finds time to help serve Communion and help with any other needs at the church. Both are active members of Trinity, Grand Island, Neb. *(LaVerne Fuller)*

Water and the Word—Little Harleigh Renee Jones is baptized by Pastor Eldon Weisheit at a baptismal font in the courtyard of church. And another child begins new life at Fountain of Life, Tucson, Ariz. *(Norman Loeber)*

There's hunger, even on Sundays. Ormonde Earp, left, and Malcomb Schnitker pick up donated baked goods from Albertson's Foods in Santa Fe, N.M., for a community hot-meal program. They are members of Immanuel, Sante Fe. *(Fred Rick)*

At the office of the Northwest District, staff member Glenn Herbold, second from left, explains the goals of the Youth Resource Consultants program. Participating in the training session are, from left, Tim Eitrein, Pilgrim, Spokane, Wash.; Herbold, director of congregational services for the district; Kelly Bailey-McCray, Trinity, Bend, Ore.; Tim Rippstein, Prince of Peace, Portland, Ore.; and Phil Meyer, St. John, Idaho Falls, Idaho. *(Sara E. Schlobohm)*

■ A spring day beckons a visit to the park. Timothy Truong, Walter Bajema, Diane Truong, Grace Bajema and David Truong enjoy Boulevard Park, Bellingham, Wash. They are members of Trinity, Bellingham. *(Carl Sahlhoff)*

■ It has been a long day for little Diane Truong and she's ready for her mother, Hoatien Truong, to take her home. They are members of Trinity, Bellingham, Wash. *(Carl Sahlhoff)*

■ Outside Redeemer, Thousand Oaks, Calif., is a barrel for members to deposit donated food items. Member Fred Fanzwa adds his contribution for the congregation's work with "Manna," the community food bank. *(Theodore R. Dibble)*

48

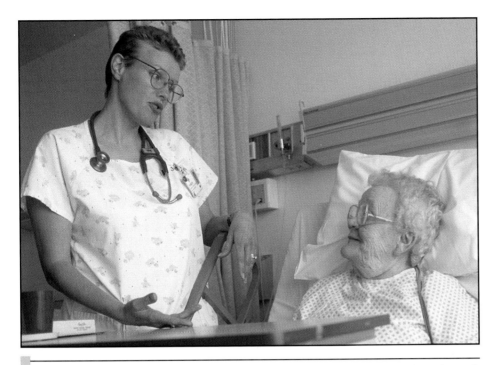

At the Marion Medical Center, Santa Maria, Calif., Janice Sigona visits with patient Edna Frambes. Janice is a member of Lutheran Church of Our Savior in Santa Maria. *(Wayne Taylor)*

Worship seems more complete when hugs and smiles are exchanged on the way home. At Greenhaven, Sacramento, Calif., Pastor William Plath hugs Linda West, a new member, following the baptism of her daughter, Erica. *(Phil Heller)*

Louisa Porter, a federal judge magistrate who helps with illegal aliens in San Diego, Calif., consults with an aide. Louisa is a member of Our Redeemer, San Diego. *(William Saxton)*

It Fitz! Isaac Schoepp balances a ring as part of his family's performance at Peace, San Diego, Calif. The Fitz family travels the country performing its balancing and juggling show—and using the opportunities to share faith in Jesus Christ. *(Rebecca Schoepp)*

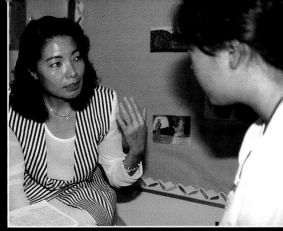

Mei Li Teller leads a Bible class in the Mandarin language at Good Shepherd, Honolulu, Hawaii. *(Wing You Tong)*

Colors of love—301 handmade quilts make their own statement as worship opens at Zion, Corvallis, Ore. The quilts, made by members, will be given to Lutheran World Relief for shipment to people in other countries. *(Sheldon Meier)*

The first outdoor baptism by Pastor Nathan Loesch at Bethany, Sacramento, Calif., brings new life to Lindsay McKenna Cerulle, as her family watches. *(Felix Rivera)*

Prayer marks the reception of new member Jan Johnson at Good Shepherd, Honolulu, Hawaii. Leading the prayer is Pastor Don Baron. *(Wing You Tong)*

It's confirmation day at Good Shepherd, Turlock, Calif. From left, Rachel Lorenzo, Kira Ehrlich, Devon Kaepernick and Adam Zuber put on their robes. *(Mel de la Motte)*

In Seaview, Wash., Lutherans share a building with Presbyterian and Episcopal congregations. Here, Pastor Harvey Buettner and Sharon and Jess Freeman remove altar and pulpit items after the Lutheran service, while choir members of the Presbyterian congregation assemble. *(Phyllis Buettner)*

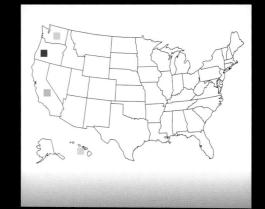

Women and children loosen the soil and pull out boulders in preparation for the school building at Wanakipa, Papua New Guinea. The new building will have a corrugated tin roof instead of the traditional thatched grass so that rain water can be gathered for drinking water during the school day. The roof also will assure that rain does not leak through and spoil papers and supplies.

Ruben walks through tall grass on his way to teaching duties at Wanakipa Lutheran School in Papua New Guinea. Funding from LCMS World Relief and congregations, plus assistance from Synod missionaries, is helping his village of Wanakipa build a new school building.

. . . whatever you do, do it all for the glory of God (1 Cor. 10:31).

Retiree Fred Kellner volunteers his time at Woodlands Lutheran Preschool in Monteverde, Fla. Samantha Poirier, left, and Katie Beth Anderson enjoy his attention. *(Kent Swanson)*

Deacon Chester Boyes is ready to go! A member of Our Redeemer, Greenville, R.I., he helps distribute food to the needy. *(Richard Droste)*

Previous page: Allison Kelly, a kindergartener at Good Shepherd Lutheran School in Elgin, Ill., jumps with all her might to clear a jump rope during recess. *(David Tonge)*

Rick Reese, a member of Concordia, Sarasota, Fla., repairs a tire at Reese Chevron, a father/son business in downtown Sarasota. *(Brenda Flegler)*

The home of Chris and Luise Christianson is the site of this Monday Bible study of the Book of James. Marcy Fleck leads the study. They all are members of Faith, Merritt Island, Fla. *(Linda Lawrence)*

Planting a tree is one way to celebrate Earth Day. Audra Lukas and several of her students at Luther Haven Day Care Center gather around the tree. The center is a program of St. Luke, Oviedo, Fla. *(John Gaudette)*

Christ, Pittsburgh, Pa., has a lot of members who enjoy walking. Peg Palascak stretches outside the church before starting her walk. *(Jessica Knoche)*

These 4-year-old preschoolers brought their favorite bears to a teddy bear picnic at Pinnacle Lutheran School in Rochester, N.Y. *(Roger Williams)*

Andrew Eckl makes finger shadows on the playground of St. Mark Lutheran School in Yonkers, N.Y. *(Andrea M. Greaney)*

"If we move this here and that there, it will work!" That's what Gilbert Thompson, an elder at St. Paul, Kingsville, Md., seems to be saying during an ad hoc meeting Monday evening. *(Timothy J. Caslow)*

Sharing hugs and laughter are a wonderful part of the day for Christine and staff member Linda Romstadt at the Luther Home of Mercy in Williston, Ohio. *(Karen Schanke)*

"I am a rose of Sharon, a lily of the valleys" (Song of Songs 2:1). The east transept of Zion, Painesville, Ohio, features the yellow rose of Sharon in the Messiah window. Messianic prophecies are shown in the six sections of the window. *(Carol Sippola)*

A two-person Lutheran radio station? Noreen Busic, right, hears through a wireless FM receiver to help Doris Brennan, director of Lutheran Metropolitan Ministries' LEAP program in Cleveland, Ohio. LEAP finds creative ways for people with severe physical disabilities to participate in and contribute to the community. Brennan is associate director of Lutheran Metropolitan Ministries. *(Joseph Karabinus)*

Organ builder Dave Wigton constructs a tracker-action organ at his shop in Dryden, Mich. He is a member of Holy Redeemer, Dryden, Mich. *(Robert L. Barker)*

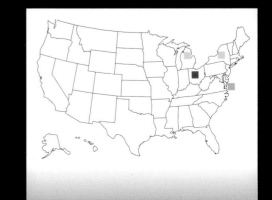

The sea gulls at Indiana Dunes State Park in Porter, Ind., enjoy this! Children from Immanuel, Michigan City, Ind., join other park visitors in feeding the gulls. *(John M. Niemann)*

Annette Grant, Carol Grant and Gudrun Olson work on quilts that will be donated to a women's shelter in Rhinelander, Wis. They are members of the Ladies Society of Our Savior, Bundy/Jeffries, Wis. *(Kurt H. Krahn)*

At Good Shepherd Lutheran School, Elgin, Ill, third grade teacher Janet Kolzow talks to a parent during parent-teacher conferences. *(David Tonge)*

Dr. David L. Huxsoll, right, Dean of the Louisiana State University School of Veterinary Medicine, confers with a senior student in the Intensive Care Unit at the school's hospital. Huxsoll is a member of Trinity Lutheran Church in Baton Rouge, La. *(Beverly A. Huxsoll)*

Jared Hammel recites the Boy Scout oath at the beginning of the weekly meeting of Troop 73 at Faith, Appleton, Wis. *(Glenn Ocock)*

It's the one-on-one conversations that are so important in everyone's life. Henry Rohling, a member of Trinity, Hammond, Ind., visits with Helen Ewen in the recreation room at the Lutheran Retirement Village in Crown Point, Ind. *(John Hassel)*

The library is full of information and activities. Marc Niemann, a member of Immanuel, Michigan City, Ind., finds relaxation in a game of checkers at the library. *(John M. Niemann)*

Even physical education classes can be fun if your friends are in class with you! From right, Kristen Wade, Lena Burns, Marissa Lewis, Andrea Lesko, Luanne Wories, Aly Wagner and Sarah Bohn are ready for class in the gym at Good Shepherd Lutheran School, Collinsville, Ill. *(Roger Etter)*

Attorney Harold M. Olsen prepares for a court case to be held at the Logan County Courthouse in Lincoln, Ill. Harold is a member of Trinity, Springfield, Ill., and a former member of the Synod's board of directors. *(Marlin W. Roos)*

Some people just love their work! Eighty-year-old Eve Malzahn types news about service times and events at St. Paul, Melrose Park, Ill., for the weekly newspaper's religion section. A valuable asset to her church, Eve has worked for many years in evangelism and publicity at the church. *(Bill Cooper)*

These students are ready to eat! From left, Debra Buss, Pam Rank and Linda Spreeman, all members of the congregation, serve lunch to students at St. Paul Lutheran School in Bonduel, Wis. *(Curt Schneider)*

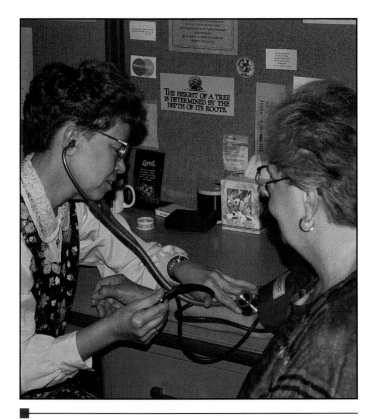

Marcia Schnorr, left, in her role as personal health counselor, takes Hetta Jeselink's blood pressure. Marcia has been the parish nurse at St. Paul, Rochelle, Ill., for 10 years. A Ph.D., she also serves as coordinator of the Synod's Parish Nurse Ministry. *(Gerald Matzke)*

"I will try to serve God . . ." That's part of the Girl Scout Promise that Brownies recite during flag ceremonies on Mondays after school at Trinity, Athens, Wis. First grade twins Megan and Melissa Gaulke are holding the flags. (By the way, Megan's on the left.) *(Bob/Sue Heckendorf)*

61

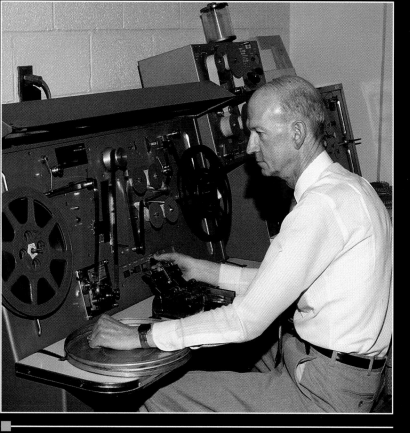

If you see a school group coming at the Illinois State Museum in Lincoln, you know Albert Casolari is behind the scenes! He inspects and cleans the movie that is shown to school groups in the museum auditorium. Albert is a member of Trinity, Springfield, Ill. *(Marlin W. Roos)*

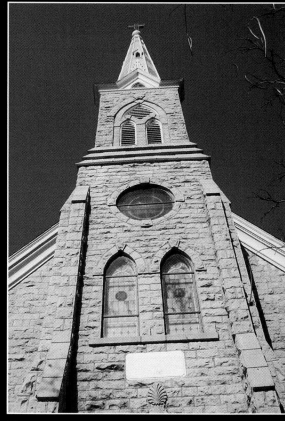

Still majestic at 156! This is a steeple view of the 156-year-old Trinity Lutheran Church in Freistadt (Mequon), Wis. *(Peter Olsen)*

A former milkhouse has become the "Loom Room" on Russell and Ruth Young's farm in Auroraville, Wis. Ruth produces hand-woven rugs from recycled fabrics to give to the needy, sell at the Second Time Around Shop (a project of area Lutheran churches) in Berlin, Wis., or sell in craft shops. Ruth and Russell are members of Immanuel, Auroraville, where he is an elder and she is past local and zone president of Lutheran Women's Missionary League. *(Nelma Stertz)*

Ancient Hebrew is easier with a computer. Senior Pastor Bob Barnes of St. Paul, Stevens Point, Wis., uses his computer to study Hebrew. *(Randy Lindemann)*

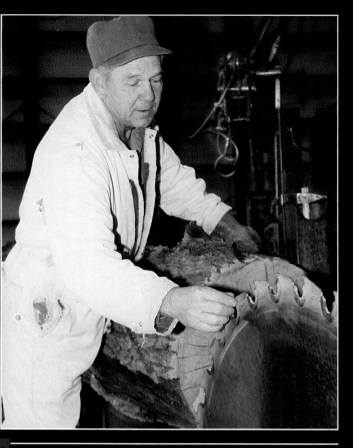

You wouldn't think there are many trees in Kansas, much less a sawmill. But Harold "Penny" Andreson checks the blades on his sawmill in Lincoln, Kan. Andreson uses oak trees harvested in Kansas to make lumber and then furniture. He's a member of St. John, Lincoln. *(Ken Greene)*

There's nothing like teamwork! These Girl Scouts, members of Trinity, Roselle, Ill., work together on a project. *(Greg Kettler)*

From one seed! Kathy Chase at Chase's Greenhouses in Rush, N.Y., shows three-year-old preschoolers how seedlings are grown commercially. They are members of Pinnacle, Rochester, N.Y. *(Roger Williams)*

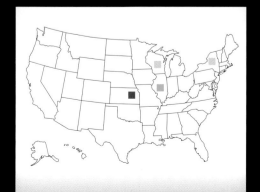

A song leader leads music for Sunday school in Almaty, Kazakstan, during a visit by a group from St. John, Fall Creek, Wis. The Almaty Sunday school plans to exchange videos and letters with the group in Fall Creek.
(Paul Bittner)

Christians from halfway around the globe join in song in Almaty, Kazakstan. Dr. Eugene Krentz (second from right) leads a song session in Almaty as a group from St. John, Fall Creek, Wis., visits. The Americans brought 175 pounds of Christian materials, translated into Russian, to share with their brothers and sisters in Kazakstan.
(Paul Bittner)

In the chemistry lab at Concordia College, Bronxville, N.Y., students Jason Cerbone and Christine Veeraraj examine the results of their research. Concordia is one of 10 colleges in the Synod's Concordia University System. *(John Warner)*

Concordia Publishing House production artist Ray Jones pauses during his job doing desktop layout of one of the 20 district editions that are produced monthly as inserts in *The Lutheran Witness*. The publishing house is in St. Louis. *(CPH)*

These girls busy themselves with a project in the extended care (after school child care) facility at Trinity, Roselle, Ill. *(Greg Kettler)*

Devotions lead the way for the Board of Education as they begin their evening meeting at St. Paul School, Perham, Minn. Principal John Gottschalk leads the group through prayer. *(Cleone Stewart)*

Beatrice Lewis operates the envelope inserter at Concordia Publishing House in St. Louis, Mo. In addition to publishing books and study material, CPH also provides mailing services for synodical departments and auxiliaries. *(CPH)*

The children were amazed when a helicopter landed on the playground of St. Paul, Truman, Minn. The D.A.R.E. officer from the Minnesota National Guard shares drug information with students and explains how the helicopter is used. On the left is Edwinna Williams (signing teacher). *(Elaine Ritz)*

Phyllis Wallace prepares another broadcast of "Woman To Woman" in the studios of Lutheran Hour Ministries in St. Louis. The program is growing in use among radio stations across the nation. *(Dave Kuenzel)*

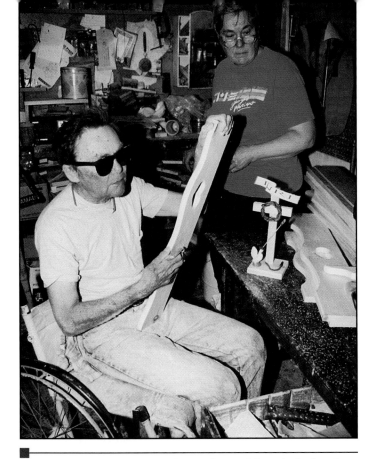

Ken Carstens doesn't let much stop him. Although he has lost his sight and both legs to diabetes, he still works in his wood-shop with the help of his wife, Linda. The Carstens are members of Gloria Dei in Virginia, Minn. *(Annette Herring)*

The last to leave the mortuary, Rev. David Marth, pastor at historic Trinity, St. Louis, Mo., pauses in private prayer at the casket of Claire Fitzgerald, who died in an auto accident April 18. The daughter of long-time Trinity members, Claire was a graduate of Lutheran schools in St. Louis and was just beginning her career as a librarian in Fayetteville, N.C. The members of Trinity gathered around the family, sharing in their loss and in their strong faith in the resurrection through their Lord Jesus. *(King Schoenfeld)*

Damien Bading, left, and William Greinke participate in the church council meeting at Mount Calvary, San Antonio, Texas. *(Robert R. Morris)*

The "First Place" Bible study, diet and exercise group at Christ Chapel, Wildwood, Mo., enjoy some humor. Facing the camera, from left: Lillian Edmiston, Eva Rau, Peggy Lancour, Peter Neuman, Sandi Heidorn-Neuman and Arline Agnew. *(Harold M. Rau)*

Physical exercise is important for the "First Place" Bible study group at Christ Chapel, Wildwood, Mo. Collectively, they have lost more than 300 pounds! *(Harold M. Rau)*

The magnificent stained glass window above the altar in the Chapel of St. Timothy and St. Titus on the campus of Concordia Seminary, St. Louis, Mo. *(Dave Kuenzel)*

Shane Olson, Kelli Parish, Jessi Rice and Emmanuel Debert—members of the high school senior youth—prepare spaghetti for members of Trinity, Guymon, Okla. *(Jo Patton)*

Michael Koch works at Woody's Welding shop in Grand Island, Neb. He's a member of Trinity, Grand Island, and a member of the school board. *(LaVern Fuller)*

Custodian Bill Maack enjoys morning sun streaming through the stained glass windows of St. Paul, West Point, Neb., as he goes about his Monday chores. *(Gwen Lindberg)*

Jessica Bickle, Zion, Columbia City, Ind., left, and her neighbor Zachary Walters, plant a sunflower in honor of the Sunday school staff at Zion. *(Barbara Knuth)*

Bruce Switzer, head elder of St. John, Burwell, Neb., runs cows for the pastor. The calves are tagged at birth for identification. (Note the tag he is using for the pastor's calf: "Holy Cow.") Burwell, the only town in Loup County, has 700 people and 50,000 cows. *(Sue Switzer)*

Keith Brogren, an elder at Salem, Gurley, Neb., witnesses with his friendly smile as he helps farmers and ranchers by hauling their hay, straw and feed. The straw, a by-product of the wheat harvest, is used for animal bedding. Most of Salem's members have jobs related to agriculture. *(Clarice Kuehn)*

Four times a year, the presidents of the Synod's 35 districts gather in St. Louis for the Council of Presidents, which also includes the president and vice-presidents of the Synod. This is the meeting when the district presidents attend call services at the seminaries in Fort Wayne and St. Louis and meet the candidates who are called to their districts. *(Suzanne Johnson)*

Henry Walter works in his garden. Nearly 96, he still drives himself and his wife to church and town. Occasionally, he'll get out his 44-year-old farm tractor to mow weeds. The Walters belong to St. John, Lincoln, Kan. *(Ken Greene)*

Todd Bethke, left, and Seth Spiegel must be looking at something very interesting through the microscope in Rebecca Lange's science class at St. Paul Lutheran School in Austin, Texas. *(Earl O. Wukasch)*

Looks good! Trudy Arnegard prepares food in Messiah's Family Life Center to be delivered to the homebound by Mobile Meals drivers from Messiah, Oklahoma City, Okla. *(Jim Cooprider)*

The chores never end! Russel Essig closes a gate on his family's ranch in North Dakota. The Essigs are members of Grace, Lehr, N.D. *(Cindy Essig)*

Pastor Craig Muhlbach and children from Salem, Gurley, Neb., remove the cross that stood outside the church during the Lenten season. It is tradition at Trinity to recycle its Christmas trees as crosses during Lent. The congregation also places a trio of similar crosses in the town park. *(Sherry Brogren)*

Family, staff and students, of Concordia St. Paul, Minn., gather for their weekly Communion service at Graebner Memorial Chapel. *(Timothy Bode)*

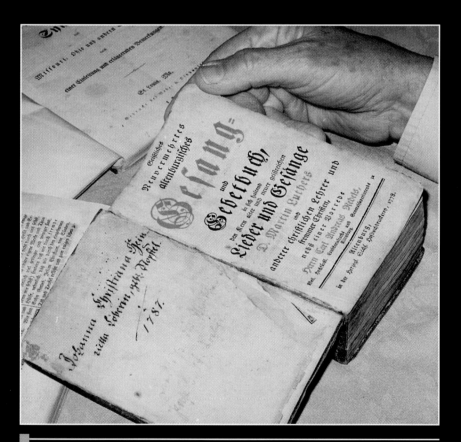

Yugi Matsumoto, a student at Concordia, Bronxville, N.Y., takes English as a Second Language. The class meets on campus at the Scheele Memorial Library. *(John Warner)*

The library of Norman C. Loeber of Tucson, Ariz., includes this 1778 Martin Luther Hymn Book. The book is part of a 150th anniversary display of old books. The Loebers are members of Fountain of Life, Tucson. *(Sally Loeber)*

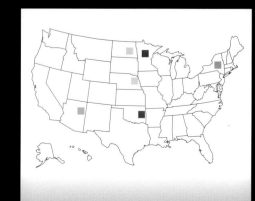

Monday evening is the time for Bible study at the Peninsula Church Center Library in Seaview, Wash. Bible study participants are Adeline and Chuck Schrantz, Jim Hill, Barbara Duensing and Pastor Harvey Buettner. They are members of St. John, Seaview. *(Phyllis M. Buettner)*

Taking care of others is something we're good at. At the Harmony Medical Center in Fort Collins, Colo., Dr. Tim Maly looks over a patient's chart with his assistant, Deb McInzie. They are members of Immanuel Lutheran Church, Loveland, Colo. *(Lani Rose Brandt)*

Helping others is just something they like to do! These preschool and kindergarten students from Trinity Lutheran School in San Rafael, Calif., walk to deliver food to a local homeless shelter's dining room. *(Barry Stueve)*

Members of the Lutheran high school conduct chapel services at the Good Shepherd Lutheran Preschool in Honolulu, Hawaii. First row, from left: Yun-Heng Chang, Timothy Li, Kelly Wu, Billy Liu, Lorien Pelletier, Jenny Hong, Derek Chan. Second row: Mike Mateo, Henry Li, Brett Will, Stephanie Gan, Jeffrey Li and Bao-Xin Chen. *(Wing You Tong)*

The children in Gretchen Fagin's preschool class at Our Savior School in Aiea, Hawaii, play with a parachute during recess. *(James A. Arendale)*

"You're outa there!" American League Umpire Tim McClelland probably has the chance to say that quite often during his job. Here he works at Jacobs Field, Cleveland, Ohio, during a game between the Cleveland Indians and the California Angels. McClelland is a member of Shepherd of the Valley, West Des Moines, Iowa. *(Ronald E. Meyer)*

Cuong Truong talks with Vietnamese children he works with in a reading program at Alderwood Elementary School in Bellingham, Wash. From left: Hue La, Timothy Truong, Lisa Huynh, Cuong Truong (seated, holding David Truong), Lieu Phan, Phuong Tran and Duong Tran. *(Carl Sahlhoff)*

Students at Trinity Preschool and Kindergarten, San Rafael, Calif., prepare to assemble a skeleton as they learn about God's creation. Trinity incorporates instructional visits from many educational agencies as part of its program. *(Barry Stueve)*

Betty Dossett, receptionist at the LCMS International Center, could be known as the "Voice of the LCMS." Her voice is the first one you hear when you call the synodical headquarters in St. Louis. *(Suzanne Johnson)*

Pastor Don Smith of Prince of Peace Lutheran Church, Tacoma, Wash., shares a conversation about Neah Bay's location and listens to the beat of a young Makah Indian drummer. Pictured with Pastor Smith is Casandra Noel, a member of the Makah Indian tribe. *(John Schmidt)*

Students work industriously at the computer lab at Our Savior Lutheran School in Aiea, Hawaii. *(James A. Arendale)*

Jan Crosby, a member of Pilgrim, Coronado, Calif., sorts mail at the Coronado Post Office. *(John C. Rumsey III)*

Singing for joy! From left, George Heath, Stacey Kahnert, Jill Henry, and Martha Schiebel at the Sommer Center, Concordia College, Bronxville, N.Y. *(John Warner)*

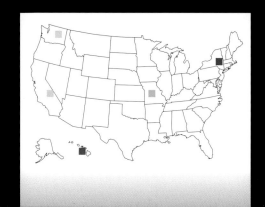

The Abiding Savior Lutheran School team from Lake Forest, Calif., wins another trophy! *(Maureen Witte)*

Delberta Novicki, Vice President for Mission Service, New England District LWML, pulls weeds at the Lutheran Home in Southbury, Conn., as part of a convention Servant Event. *(Peg Huebner)*

Donna Petersen, left, and Lois Koeske make calls as part of the prayer chain ministry of Redeemer Lutheran Church, Thousand Oaks, Calif. *(Theodore R. Dibble)*

There are different kinds of service, but the same Lord (1 Cor. 12:5).

Lori Welch and Lori LeDuc, auditors from the Synod's offices in St. Louis, Mo., conduct an audit of Woodlands Lutheran Ministries in Montverde, Fla. *(Kent Swanson)*

Banners are a common sight in Lutheran churches everywhere! These banners are suspended from the balcony at St. John, Depew, N.Y. *(Michael Blackwell)*

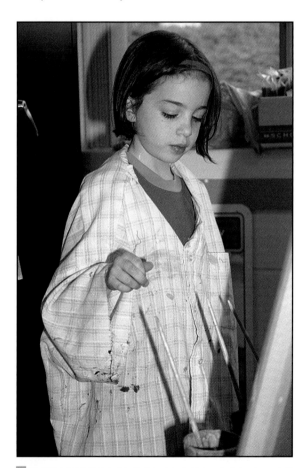

Maureen Griffin, a student of Good Shepherd Christian Preschool, State College, Pa., paints at an easel. *(Marcus Voth)*

Foreign-born students in the kindergarten class of Pinnacle Lutheran School, Rochester, N.Y., are showing the other children where their home countries are on the world globe. *(Roger Williams)*

Previous page: A labor of love! That's what these quilters call the work they do. Top, from left, are Irene Liescheidt and Fern Stewart. Florence Meyer is in the foreground. All are members of Trinity, Pekin, Ill. *(Jim Deverman)*

It's food for the body and food for the soul. Every Tuesday morning, Rob Grady, foreground, director of Christian education at Trinity, Lombard, Ill., leads the men's Bible breakfast at a local restaurant. *(Bill Cooper)*

Teresa Ovaert uses the rounder in the large-muscle area of Good Shepherd Preschool in State College, Pa. *(M. H. Voth)*

Ralph Davis stands guard, ready to help school children safely cross the street in Seattle, Wash. Ralph is a member of Good Shepherd, Seattle. *(Lisa D. Brown)*

81

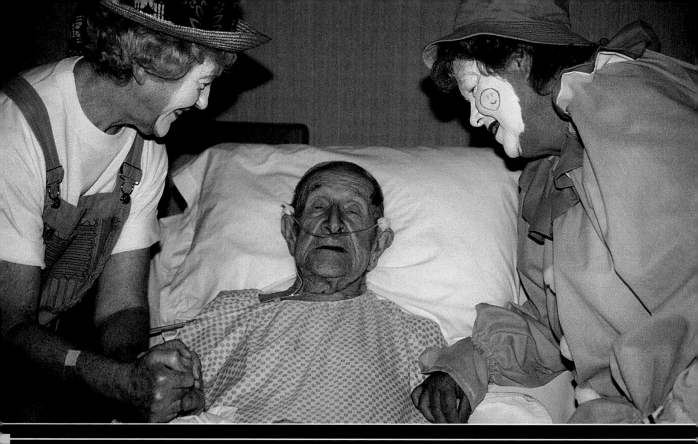

Clowns from the Clown Ministry of Grace, Destin, Fla., brighten the day of 95-year-old Art McDaniels, a member of Good Shepherd, Shalimar, Fla., and a resident of the Manor at Bluewater Bay, Niceville. *(Bea Daily)*

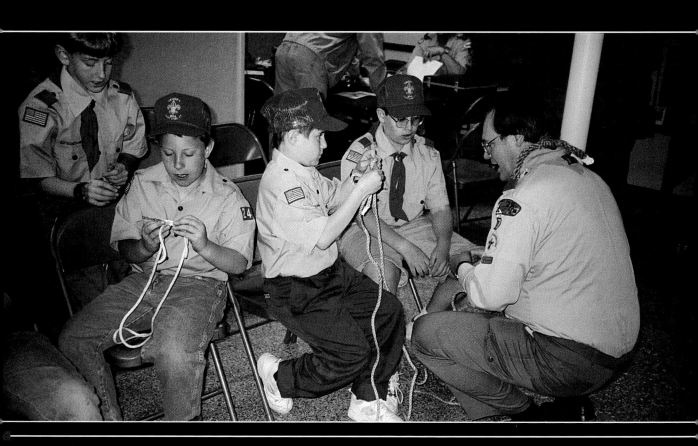

Over and under ... Scoutmaster Gary McCue, right, teaches the finer points of knot-making to, from left, Tim Moller, Jason aPlant, Ian Groom and Pat King. The Scouts meet at Christ, Niantic, Conn. *(Peg Huebner)*

Employees at the LCMS International Center, St. Louis, Mo., enjoy lunch in the cafeteria. The colorful flags represent each country where the Synod has a mission relationship. They remind them and us that our Synod is active worldwide. *(Suzanne Johnson)*

Pastor Russell Frahm of Faith, Merritt Island, Fla., brings the Lord's Supper to homebound member Herman Mueller. *(Linda Lawrence)*

Members of Christ the King, Largo, Fla., compile a 25-minute videotape of the worship service for broadcast twice a week on a public service cable television station. The editors are former congregation presidents Don Lochner, left, and Norm Hesterman. They took a special training course at the studio for this modern missionary service, which brings the Word through television. *(Gwen Diller)*

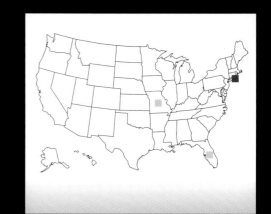

Kathy Schamber prepares to escort her Baton Rouge, La., Lutheran School first graders to the carpool site at the end of the school day. Kathy is also president-elect of the Lutheran Education Association's Department of Early Childhood Education. *(Beverly A. Huxsoll)*

Students head for class at Concordia University, Portland, Ore. From left, Alison Ludke, Melissa Bond and Heather Kaufman. *(Vern Uyetake)*

Roger Vernick checks Bible references in preparation for an evangelism training session at Zion, Painesville, Ohio. *(Carol Sippola)*

"Hey, Mom!" Kaytlin Fitzgerald finds something she wants to buy at the thrift store operated by Good News Ministries in Whittemore, Mich. *(Janet Keinath)*

Rev. Mark Kloha tapes a weekly radio program, "When You Need a Friend," for broadcast on station WTCR in Catlettsburg, Ky. Kloha is pastor of St. Paul, Ashland, Ky. *(Mary H. Robinson)*

Bev Christiansen of the Lutheran Family Service in Fort Dodge, Iowa, helps Chris Kjolhede plan his living expenses and budget his income for the month. *(Kenneth A. Hays)*

Merril Jacobsen reassembles the organ in Immanuel's new church, Freeport, Ill. *(Lynn Hoefle)*

Family and friends make their way to the chapel for the vicarage assignment service at Concordia Theological Seminary in Fort Wayne, Ind. *(Gerald Matzke)*

At the conclusion of the vicarage placement service at Concordia Theological Seminary, Fort Wayne, Ind., family members race to find one another and learn the details of their placement. Here seminarian Grant Knepper and his wife, Pam, look over the documents. *(Gary Penner)*

Chaplain Edward Johnson, center, is joined by visiting seafarers from Greece, left, and the Philippines, right, at the Seafarer's Center in Commencement Bay, Tacoma, Wash. *(John Schmidt)*

Forrest Alderson, of the Distribution Department at Concordia Publishing House, St. Louis, Mo. Soon Forrest will mark his 28th anniversary with the publishing company which was founded in 1869. *(CPH)*

From the Dunes Park Station in Chesterton, Ind., Joe Broad calls an "All aboard!" A member of Immanuel, Michigan City, Ind., he is a conductor for the Chicago South Bend/South Shore Railroad. *(John M. Niemann)*

Can't wait to come to school! Jonathan Lau, in front, Chris Sahs, right and Scott Sahs get off the bus—ready to start another day at Zion School in Hinsdale, Ill. *(Ruta Jensen)*

Tom Nummela, the editor of youth materials at Concordia Publishing House in St. Louis, works on new junior high Sunday school lessons. He is a member of Salem, Affton, Mo. *(Jane L. Haas)*

"School Dad" John Ninke digs a hole for the chinning bar on the playground of Grace Lutheran School, Killeen, Texas. *(Tim Matthys)*

Rod Grams, U.S. Senator from Minnesota, speaks to a school group in Washington, D.C. Grams attends Living Christ in Chanhassen, Minn. *(Tom Swanson)*

Costumed children at Trinity School, St. Louis, Mo., wait nervously backstage for the curtain to rise on their annual "Kids Praise" performance. Out front, parents with video cameras, younger children and congregation members wait eagerly. The school, opened in 1839, is the oldest continually operated elementary school in the St. Louis area. *(King Schoenfeld)*

Grandmother Carolyn Langbecker gives her grandson, Jacob Langbecker, help during a "Together with Jesus" Sunday school class for two-year-olds at St. John, Arnold, Mo. *(Jane L. Haas)*

An editor's work is never done! Jane L. Fryar, an editor in curriculum development at Concordia Publishing House, outlines devotional readings for "Today's Light." She is a member of Ascension, St. Louis, Mo. *(Jane L. Haas)*

A New Career—Pastor

About six years ago, Keith Besel decided to change careers: from business management to pastor. With the support of his wife, Mary Beth, the family moved from Colorado to Seward, Neb., so he could complete his pre-seminary studies at Concordia College.

He and his family, which included daughter, Brittnie, and son, Travis, in addition to his wife, then relocated to St. Louis, Mo., so Keith could begin studies at Concordia Seminary.

The pictures on these two pages show the Besel family, which now includes daughter Kierstyn, on Call Day, April 23. *(Photos by Paul Ockrassa)*

Keith spent a lot of time in study over the last few years as he prepared to become a pastor of The Lutheran Church—Missouri Synod.

During Keith's last year of study at Concordia Seminary, the Besel family lived at the new Concordia Woods area on the seminary grounds.

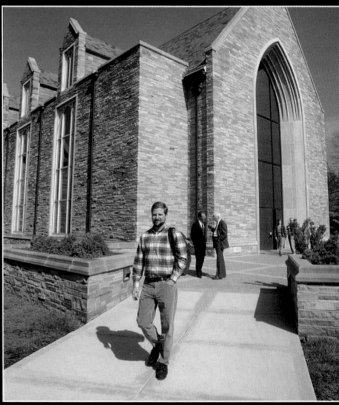

Keith has made this walk many times. He's on the Concordia Seminary campus in St. Louis. In the background is the Chapel of St. Timothy and St. Titus.

It's an important day for the Besel family. After six years of study (pre-seminary and seminary), four moves (to Seward, Neb.; to St. Louis; to Nebraska for vicarage; and back to St. Louis for a final year of study), Keith and Mary Beth are anxious and happy that Call Day has finally arrived.

Keith receives his Call to Superior Lutheran Church, Superior, Colo. On the left is Dr. John Heins, president of the LCMS Michigan District and chairman of the Council of Presidents. Rev. David Smith, the seminary's Dean of Student Life and Director of Placement, is pictured in the center.

The Call service takes place in the majestic Chapel of St. Timothy and St. Titus on the seminary's campus.

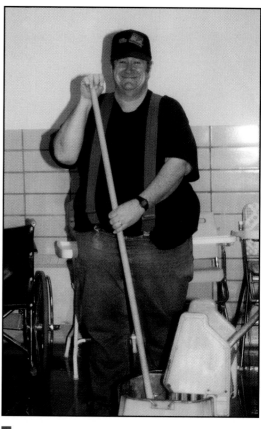

Inez Allen learns to prepare food inexpensively through Project Strength—a ministry of St. Luke, Kansas City, Kan. *(Judith McGuire)*

Ron Jackson, church and school custodian at Trinity in Boone, Iowa, stands at the rear of the parish hall. He's always happy when the floor cleaning and polishing job is done! *(Sharon Witcraft)*

Police officer Dana Kuster and Iowa Highway Patrolman Greg Hall talk in a parking lot. Dana and Greg are members of Faith, Mount Pleasant, Iowa. *(Paul Meyer)*

Jim Turbes talks with a caller during his call-in show on KWBG radio station in Boone, Iowa. Jim, a newscaster and general announcer at KWBG, is a member of Trinity in Boone. *(Sharon Witcraft)*

First grade teacher Carla Niemeier guides her students through a project at Trinity, Clinton Township, Mich. *(David Tirsell)*

Singing is an integral part of our lives. Here, Melanie Maddick and her third through eighth graders from Clemons School in State Center, Iowa, practice for an operetta: "Living on the Edge." *(Bonnie Berrey)*

It's too nice to be inside on a day like this! Rachel Wapelhorst, St. Paul School, West Point, Neb., takes her books outdoors.
(Gwen Lindberg)

93

Don Diestelmeier is staining the inside of the cabinet that holds the pipes for the organ at Immanuel, Freeport, Ill. A couple of pipes are already in place inside the cabinet. *(Lynn Hoefle)*

Carl Tobiason has been working with stained glass since 1953. He worked on the windows at St. Paul in St. Joseph, Mo., and has worked on many other churches in Missouri and Nebraska. *(Greg Beechner)*

Animals are a wonderful part of God's creation! Seven-year-old Rebecca Heinze carefully touches a chick. She's a member of St. John, Lincoln, Kan. *(Ken Greene)*

Paula Covey and her son Eric are active participants in the "Moms in Touch" program at St. Paul School, Austin, Texas, praying for the concerns of the school and church. *(Mark Matson)*

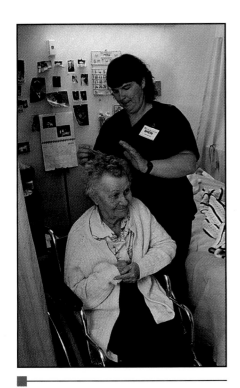

Sheri Suelter gives loving care to resident Lucille Panzer at the Mid-America Nursing Home in Lincoln, Kan. *(Ken Greene)*

Marty Imler opens her home to these women who study the Bible together. They are members of Emmanuel (Soest), Fort Wayne, Ind. *(Greg Messmann)*

The campus of Prince of Peace, Carrollton, Texas, was formerly the site of the world's largest auto mall. With ample parking, the congregation uses the buildings for a worship center, day school, youth activities and other functions. *(Karen Eggemeyer)*

A musical group rehearses in the sanctuary of Prince of Peace, Carrollton, Texas. *(Karen Eggemeyer)*

First grade friends enjoy learning about Jesus during midweek class at Trinity, Port Arthur, Texas. From left, Samantha Myers, Joshua Harris, Tennisha Gothia, Thuy Nguyen and Giau Chiem. *(Nancy Dinger)*

Lutherans are involved in many kinds of work around the world. A member of Gloria Dei, Houston, Texas, Amy Reynolds works as a government liaison with NASA. *(Thomas N. Van Duzer)*

Glenn Pogue takes his place as NASA does a mission control test for the space shuttle in Houston, Texas. Glenn is a member of Gloria Dei, Houston. *(Thomas N. Van Duzer)*

Debbie Ascher and her daughter, Caitlin, raise these beautiful golden retrievers. They're pictured on the playground of Immanuel Lutheran School in Loveland, Colo. *(Lani Rose Brandt)*

Yvonne Reinke is school secretary at Clover Trinity, Buhl, Idaho. Here she enjoys a midday break with the Scriptures and contemplation. *(Robert J. MacDonald)*

School is fun, for the fifth grade class at Trinity Lutheran School, Lansing, Ill. *(Gene Brackman)*

Sally Loeber, a stained glass artist is in her studio, designing a new window for Fountain of Life, Tucson, Ariz. *(Norman Loeber)*

Dress rehearsal of the handbell choir at Our Savior, Cupertino, Calif., finds bell ringers Janet Brishin, left, and Michelle Bestul in deep concentration as they ring praises. *(Earl Davidson)*

Leland Frese is choir director and teacher at Our Savior, Cupertino, Calif. Here he directs the handbell choir. *(Earl Davidson)*

Janelle Heine feeds shell corn to her sheep on the farm that she and her husband, John, operate near Waverly, Iowa. Janelle uses the income from the small flock to pay tuition for her sons at the Lutheran school. The Heines are members of St. Paul, Artesian, Waverly, Iowa. *(Kathleen Scott)*

Practice makes perfect! Caitlin Wilkes, left, and Amy Hamilton learn how to be acolytes at Redeemer, Atascadero, Calif. *(Bonnie Pixley)*

Martha Moriarty enjoys the daffodils brought to her in the hospital by fellow member Helen Darling. Both women are members of First Trinity, Oakland, Calif. *(William Nettle)*

At Concordia Gospel Ministry in Bangkok, Thailand, in back, from left, Ruth Van Zandt, Michelle Miller and Cheryl Ehlers observe craft time at the CGM Center English camp. *(Jeff Ehlers)*

Pamela Boehle-Silva keeps the congregation informed by posting an event on the Health Ministries bulletin board at Holy Cross, Rocklin, Calif. *(William Bauer)*

At the Sneed home school, teacher-mom Veda Sneed works with her son, Isaiah, matching color-coded block letters. The Sneeds are members of Good Shepherd, Seattle, Wash. *(Lisa D. Brown)*

9 x 8 equals ?? Jacob, left, and David Sneed work hard together on their math lesson. *(Lisa D. Brown)*

Willing hands of friends make the job easier. St. John, Seaview, Wash., members Sharon, Randy and young Jesse Freeman, along with their pastor, Rev. Harvey Buettner, help spread gravel on Jim Hill's driveway in Long Beach, Wash. *(Phyllis M. Buettner)*

Darlene Burridge assists synodical church workers in Worker Benefit Plans at the Synod's International Center, in St. Louis, Mo. *(Suzanne Johnson)*

Royal Fan, Jiamian and Pastor Daniel Lee, members of Prince of Peace, Tacoma, Wash. *(John Schmidt)*

Pastor Daniel Lee, Andy Ma, Janet Au and Leo Lai touch up the display for the Easter season. They are members of Prince of Peace, Tacoma, Wash. *(John Schmidt)*

Members of Good Shepherd, Seattle, Wash., study the Scriptures in their home prayer group. From left, host Alcine Wyatt, Stella Nash, Barbara Williams, Ralph Davis, Ruth Bacalzo and DeLois Lofton. *(Lisa D. Brown)*

Young Jiamian participates in a Chinese language program, an outreach of the Beacon Asian Lutheran Mission, Seattle, Wash. *(John Schmidt)*

Students at the South Central Seminary in Wuhan, China, take time off from their studies to wash their clothes. *(Henry Rowold)*

The daughter of Rev. Zhu of Yichang church plays the zheng, a traditional Chinese instrument. *(Henry Rowold)*

Dr. Henry Rowold, left, answers questions during break time at South Central Seminary in Wuhan, China.

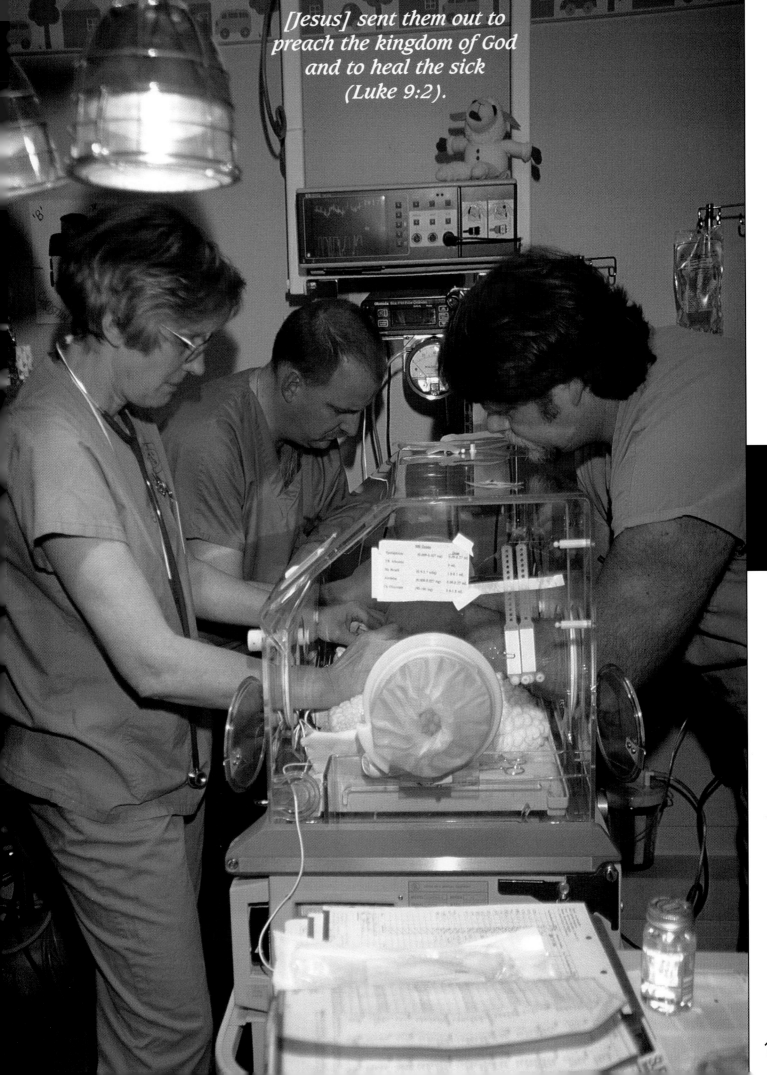

[Jesus] sent them out to preach the kingdom of God and to heal the sick (Luke 9:2).

Anna McGinn, a member of Trinity, New Hyde Park, N.Y., stitches a quilt for Lutheran World Relief. *(Yvonne Schmidt)*

Emily Hagen and Cody Rachels help out during the Wednesday morning chapel service at Faith Lutheran Preschool, Merritt Island, Fla. *(Linda Lawrence)*

Previous page:
The medical staff at Swedish Hospital, Seattle, Wash., tends to Christian James Richardson, the heaviest (2 pounds, 3 ounces) of the quadruplets born to John and Roxanne Richardson of Hoquiam, Wash. The Richardsons are members of Prince of Peace, Tacoma. *(John Schmidt)*

Preschool director Laurie Hartner sported a down-home look for Farm Day at St. Paul Child Enrichment Center, Fort Lauderdale, Fla. Laurie is married to Timothy Hartner, St. Paul's pastor. *(Marsha L. Holm)*

The courtyard at Concordia, Sarasota, Fla., provides a comfortable environment for Pastor Edward DeWitt's confirmation class. Members include, from left, Danny Williams, Patrick DeWitt, Larry Edwards, Ritchie Coiro, Melissa Gutzmer, Carrie Hysell, Nicole Bothast, Keely Taylor and Jennifer Crady, partially hidden by Pastor DeWitt. *(Brenda Flegler)*

Second-year seminarians at Concordia Theological Seminary, Fort Wayne, Ind., eagerly look over the order of service before the vicarage placement service. Where will they spend the coming year? From left, are Jim Coffey, Carl Brown, Jerald Dulas, Paul Duffy and Karl Bollhagen. *(Gary Penner)*

Members of the St. Peter, Brooklyn, N.Y. youth group package personal care items for elderly residents at Wartburg Lutheran Home in Brooklyn. From left, are Pastor Derek Taylor, Julie Taylor, Liston Gillette, Sergio Franqui and Clara Del Valle. *(Judith Benke)*

Mrs. Camp and pre-kindergarten students at Grace, Vestal, N.Y., dressed paper dolls in clothes resembling Joseph's coat-of-many-colors. *(Gerlinde U. Repinecz)*

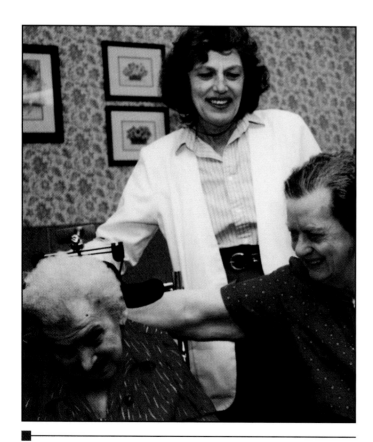

At the Hazleton Geriatric Center, residents Mary Mariano, left, and Mildred Fischer, right, enjoy break time with registered nurse Joan Denesevich. Joan is a member of St. John, Hazleton, Pa. *(Lil Junas)*

Grandparents Day at St. Paul Lutheran School, Glen Burnie, Md., provided an opportunity for first graders to practice their reading skills. Joan and James Young eagerly listen as Paul Susek and granddaughter Brittany Benson read to them. *(Patricia Lee Napora)*

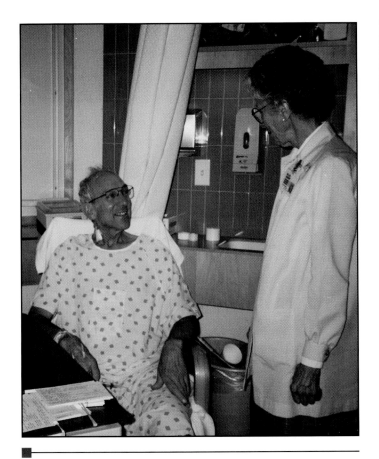

Students in the upper grades of Trinity Lutheran School, Clinton Township, Mich., pitched in during Earth Week to plant a tree on the church property. This was the 37th tree that students added to Trinity's landscape in recent years. Each tree planted honors a longtime member. *(David Tirsell)*

Helen Graber, a volunteer in the chaplain's office at University Hospital, enjoys visiting with patients. She is a member of St. John, South Euclid, Ohio. *(Doris Gillenwater)*

Melissa Nichols easily clears the bar in the high jump competition at Smithfield High School, Smithfield, R.I. She is a member of Our Redeemer, Greenville, R.I. *(Richard Droste)*

Melissa Nichols, second from left, watches the track competition with teammates and friends at Smithfield High School, Smithfield, R.I. Melissa is a member of Our Redeemer, Greenville, R.I. *(Richard Droste)*

109

Nellie Harrison, of Redeemer, Cleveland, Ohio, discusses infant nutrition at Redeemer's Hunger Center. Redeemer no longer has a pastor and may discontinue as a congregation. The future of its Hunger Center is also unknown. *(Deborah Phillips)*

Shontay Freeny, a bookstore clerk at Concordia Publishing House, St. Louis, Mo., is always ready to give friendly assistance to shoppers. *(CPH)*

Fourth-year seminarian Ralph and Sue Abernethy share their excitement in learning about their first Call. Ralph was awarded the Abdel Ross Wentz Prize for excellence in historical research and writing in American Lutheranism. The Call service was held at St. Paul, Fort Wayne, Ind. *(Gary Penner)*

Sharing her gift of music, Jane Hood Smith is an organist at St. Paul, Ashland, Ky., and leads the church choir. *(Mary H. Robinson)*

Learning is fun when Lisa Mull, teacher at St. Peter, Columbus, Ind., plays the guitar. *(Tim Ostrander)*

St. Paul, a country church in Denham, Ind., wears its 123 years well. Recently the interior was plastered, painted and decorated. *(Mildred Redweik)*

Captive Free band members Dave Anderson and Marla Doehling read mail from home on their day off at St. Peter, Columbus, Ind. *(Tim Ostrander)*

Sisters Kristen and Katelyn Moore like to help their daddy, Steve, take care of pigs on his farm near Camp Point, Ill. Although there is one year difference in their ages, they often are mistaken for twins. Katelyn will be in her father's Sunday school class next year at Good Shepherd, Clayton.
(Roger G. Buss)

Oklahoma Wildcat fan Sharon Haines concentrates on her music during choir practice at St. Paul, Ashland, Ky.
(Mary Robinson)

The bathtub is a popular reading spot in Lisa Mull's classroom at St. Peter Lutheran School, Columbus, Ind. *(Tim Ostrander)*

Registration and an open house at Trinity Preschool at Hammond, Ind., offered children and parents an opportunity to see—and sample—the facilities. *(John Hassel)*

Velma Buuck completes a quilt one stitch at a time at Zion, Friedheim, Ind. *(Addy Schuller)*

At Zion Lutheran Preschool in Garrett, Ind., teacher's aide Chris Hall helps Jennifer Cole read a word in the book she just checked out. Michelle Neukom awaits her turn. *(Julie Faulkner)*

From the capitol steps in Washington, D.C., eighth graders from St. Peter Lutheran School, Macomb, Mich., listen intently to U.S. Senator Abraham of Michigan. *(Dave Winningham)*

At the Cherry Lane Apartments on the campus of Michigan State University in Lansing, Pan Pan is working on a craft project during Bible class. She is from China. *(Petr Klan)*

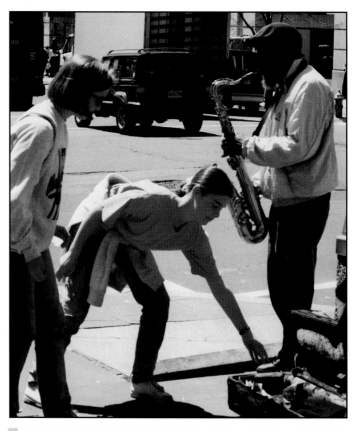

Megan Powe watches Sarah Chapman throw a dollar in the case of a saxophone player along the street in Washington, D.C. He later played "Jesus Loves Me." The girls, students at St. Peter Lutheran School, Macomb, Mich., traveled to the nation's capital as part of their eighth grade class trip. *(Dave Winningham)*

Wilma Stocker, a nurse and director of nursing, takes the pulse of Olga Buckstagge, a resident of The Christian Village Nursing Home in Lincoln, Ill. Both women are members at Zion Lutheran Church in Lincoln.
(Marlin W. Roos)

Michael Furhman and his cat check out the cattle on the family's farm near Fairbanks, Wis. He's a member of St. John, Tigerton, Wis. *(Cindy Mueller)*

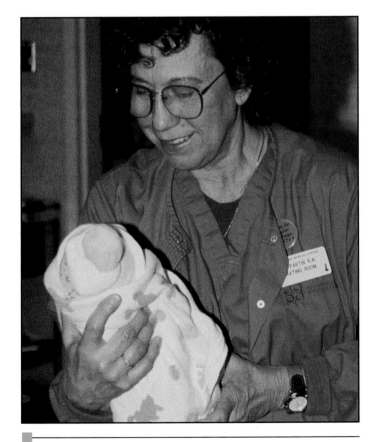

This is the Wyneken House, where F. C. D. Wyneken lived from 1859–64 when he served as synodical president. It is located half a mile from Zion Friedheim Church in northwest Adams County, Ind. It is one of the oldest existing synodical landmarks. Wyneken served as president from 1850–64.
(Addy Schuller)

Barb Partin, of Zion, Akron, Ohio, comforts a newborn baby at the New Life Center, Akron General Medical Center, in Akron.
(Christine McCune)

Giving new definition to the term "Hell's Angels," the clergy of St. Paul, West Point, Neb., take their secretary and parish coordinator out to lunch in Beemer for Secretary's Day. From left are secretary Shari Reeson, Associate Pastor Nick Wirtz, parish coordinator Ardie Smith and Senior Pastor Gregg Hein. *(Gwen Lindberg)*

Dr. Wesley T. Osthus, a member of Christ Lutheran Church, Clinton, Ill., stands by a mural of Noah's Ark that decorates a wall in the waiting room of his veterinary office in Clinton. *(Marlin W. Roos)*

Quilters at St. Paul, Stevens Point, Wis., mix fellowship and service at a quilt-making session. *(Randy Lindemann)*

The focal point of this classroom at St. Paul, Sheboygan Falls, Wis., is the cross, decorated for spring by girls in the primary department. *(Lorraine C. Wilson)*

After a time of songs and corporate prayer during a service at Faith, Geneva, Ill., worshipers separated into small groups for prayer. Here, Art Simonson, left, and Herbert Keers join hands to pray for one another. *(Bill Cooper)*

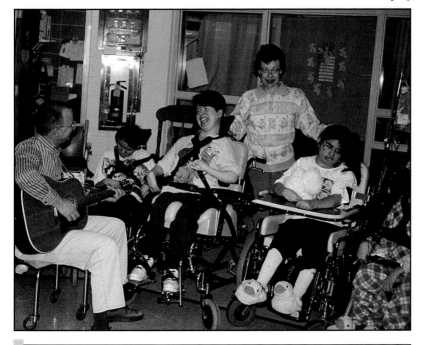

Residents of Marklund Children's Home in Bloomingdale, Ill., enjoy learning about God's love through music at Wednesday School, led by Rev. Don Kretzschmar, Northern Illinois District chaplain, left. Alice Zoelick, standing behind residents, is a member of St. Peter, Schaumberg, and a volunteer at the home. *(Diane L. Mueller)*

Machael Cleveland, at the piano, directs a rehearsal of the IC Ensemble. The group of employees at the Synod's International Center in St. Louis, Mo., regularly provides gospel music for morning chapel. Standing, from left, are Linda Rupert, Helen Evans, Dorcas Haynes, Debra Hurst, April Hughes and Lee Townsend. *(Suzanne Johnson)*

Having fun at the confirmands' pizza party in the St. Paul fellowship hall, Perham, Minn., are these daughters of Pastor Terry and Nancy Grzybowski. *(Cleone Stewart)*

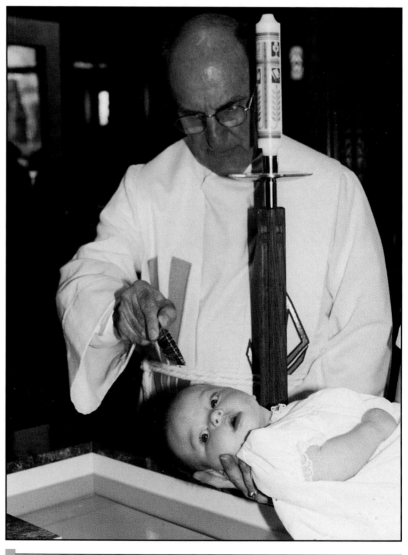

Dr. Robert Jacobson of the Public Health Service serves as director of the Hansen's Disease Center in Carville, La. The center is the only one of its kind to treat victims of leprosy. The center became famous as the subject of the book *Miracle at Carville.* Jacobson is a member of Trinity, Baton Rouge. *(Beverly Huxsoll)*

Pastor Richard Nack of St. Paul, Sheboygan Falls, Wis., baptizes a precious new life, a new member of the family of God. *(Lorraine C. Wilson)*

Pastor David Albertin, Immanuel, Michigan City, Ind., videotapes a program for a local cable channel. He regularly finds interesting ways to explain God's Law and Gospel to audiences who are not familiar with the Word. *(John Niemann)*

A number of employees of a St. Louis-based aeronautical company are members of several area LCMS congregations. They stand in front of the mock-up of a new single engine jet.

In Washington, D.C., Dan Meyer, LCMS member, is an assistant to Newt Gingrich. *(Tom Swanson)*

Rev. David Adams, left, executive director of the Synod's Office of Government Information in Washington, D.C., meets with Illinois Sen. Paul Simon. *(Tom Swanson)*

In a congressional committee room in the Longsworth Building, Nebraska Congressman Doug Bereuter, a member of St. Paul, Utica, Neb., meets with students from his home district to discuss issues, answer questions and explain how Congress works. *(Tom Swanson)*

Sing to the Lord a new song. These young girls join in singing praise during the chapel service at St. Paul, Perham, Minn. *(Cleone Stewart)*

Jim Schrieber, a member of Holy Cross, Eureka, Mont., plants yellowstone cutthroat trout in Tetrault Lake. *(Richard Payton)*

Every Wednesday morning, volunteer Muriel Armbrecht works in the Clemons Lutheran School Library, checking in books and helping students make selections. She is a member at St. John, State Center, Iowa. *(Bonnie Berrey)*

For 150 years, men have studied at Concordia Theological Seminary. Tonight, at St. Paul, Fort Wayne, Ind., 77 men step forward to receive their Calls. *(Gary Penner)*

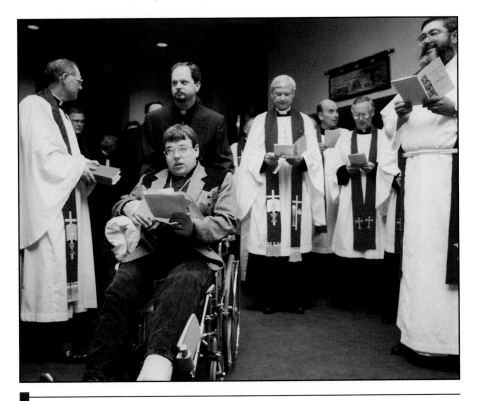

Doctor of Missiology student Dan Harmelink lends a helping hand to seminarian Mark Hass as they enter St. Paul, Fort Wayne, Ind. The students will receive their first Calls into the pastoral ministry of The Lutheran Church—Missouri Synod. Far left is Dr. William Weinrich, interim president of Concordia Theological Seminary. At right are professors Kurt Marquart, Heino Kadai, Richard Muller and Lane Burgland. *(Gary Penner)*

Family members have mixed emotions, and tears sometimes mingle with laughter in the anxious moments before Concordia Theological Seminary's Call service begins at St. Paul, Fort Wayne, Ind. Alexis and Angela Miille wait to learn where their dad, Tim Miille, will be called. *(Gary Penner)*

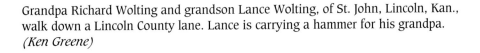

Grandpa Richard Wolting and grandson Lance Wolting, of St. John, Lincoln, Kan., walk down a Lincoln County lane. Lance is carrying a hammer for his grandpa. *(Ken Greene)*

At Mount Olive, Miami, Okla., students practice for worship under the direction of Tom Mangus, Miami School Band director and an elder of Mount Olive. From left, are Jessica Lindemeier, Deandra Boyer, Laura Botts, Katie Botts and Tom Mangus. *(Gary Boehne)*

Bob Catherwood and Sue Catherwood check their pistols prior to competition shooting at the county pistol range in Santa Fe, N.M. The Catherwoods are members at Immanuel, Santa Fe. *(Fred Rick)*

Pancakes are especially tasty when cooked in the orange groves near Yuma, Ariz. Helen and Ivan Miller of Calvary, Yuma, are part of the "Lunch Bunch," a group of retirees who meet weekly for Bible study and lunch (and sometimes breakfast!). *(Rhoda Wahl)*

From one generation to the next: The confirmation class, all eighth graders, of Prince of Peace, Tacoma, Wash., visits the congregation's most senior member, Marcella Huber, age 96. From left to right: Amanda Guill, Melissa Shaw and Jessica Schmidt. *(John Schmidt)*

Frances Krummenheck, a member of Immanuel, Santa Fe, N.M., looks at a banner that will be used to celebrate the Synod's 150th anniversary. *(Fred Rick)*

Christ, Yuma, Ariz., and all God's people who worship there, will benefit from the efforts and hard work of Laborers For Christ. Laying blocks for new sanctuary walls are Ned Face and Gene Hafner. *(Rhoda Wahl)*

The Stroilov family made this globe to use in home schooling their children. Pointing out Kharkov, Ukraine, where the family came from, are Andrey Stroilov, 9, and Olga Stroilov, 11. The family lives in Bellingham, Wash., and worships at Trinity Lutheran Church. *(Carl Sahlhoff)*

Laborers For Christ, mostly retired tradesmen, volunteer with their building skills. They are building parapet walls on a new sanctuary for Christ, Yuma, Ariz. From left, Bob Shelton, Vaughn Betts, Al Conaway and Ned Face. *(Rhoda Wahl)*

Meeting in a member's home for fellowship and Bible study are from left, Rong-Hui Xu, Yuan Wong, Jenny Wong, Xin Lin and IaMei Baron, members of Good Shepherd, Honolulu, Hawaii. *(Wing You Tong)*

Marge and Mike Thiel pause for a quick photo as they prepare bags of groceries at Redeemer Hunger Center, Redeemer, Cleveland, Ohio. *(Deborah Phillips)*

Members of Ethel Rudolph's Bible class meet for singing and study in Lucas Hall at Christ, La Mesa, Calif. In front are Freda Breise, left, and Edna Lucas. *(Jane Thompson)*

John Kreitzer coordinates religious activities and here talks over a Bible story with resident Beverly Barnett at the Good Shepherd home in Porterville, Calif. Beverly attends Zion in Terra Bella. Good Shepherd Lutheran Home of the West, Terra Bella, Calif., serves more than 700 people with mental retardation in five states. *(Raymond Cauwet)*

Attending midweek school at teacher Debbie Mack's house are, from left, Veronica Longley, Angela Mach, Carissa Trotter, Brittany Bailey and Tammy Moris, all members of Denali Lutheran Church, Anderson, Alaska. *(Ruth Zeller)*

First grader Lydia Allen narrates a part of the chapel service at Ascension Lutheran School, Torrance, Calif. *(Carol Geisler)*

Persons of all ages attend handbell choir practice at St. John, Lone Wolf, Okla. Sandra Geis conducts while daughter Monica makes a quick getaway down the aisle. *(Willard G. Wegner)*

Debra, second from left, and Gerald Fisher, kneeling, of Faith, Appleton, Wis., have visited Raja and Mahmud Khatib, standing right, and their four children in Jerusalem. The Khatibs now live in Appleton. Here the two families enjoy a reunion. The Khatib children are from left, Samer, Kamel, behind tree, Sami and Abed. *(Bob Mickelson)*

Good sound quality comes under the watchful eyes and ears of Dave Gehlhar, chief of sound production and engineering for St. Luke, Westminster, Calif. *(Larry Smith)*

Hayley Jo Hoover bows her head for a moment of prayer before class begins at Concordia Lutheran School, Seattle, Wash. *(T. Bird)*

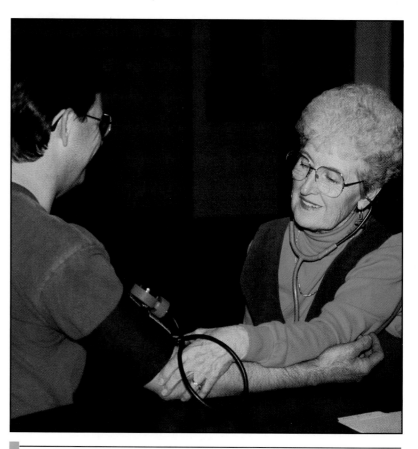

Parish nurse Nancy Smith checks the blood pressure of Neil Doop at Faith, East Wenatchee, Wash. *(Shirley Porter)*

Pastor Ron Youngdale of Good Shepherd, Turlock, Calif., prepares his Sunday morning sermon. *(Mel de la Motte)*

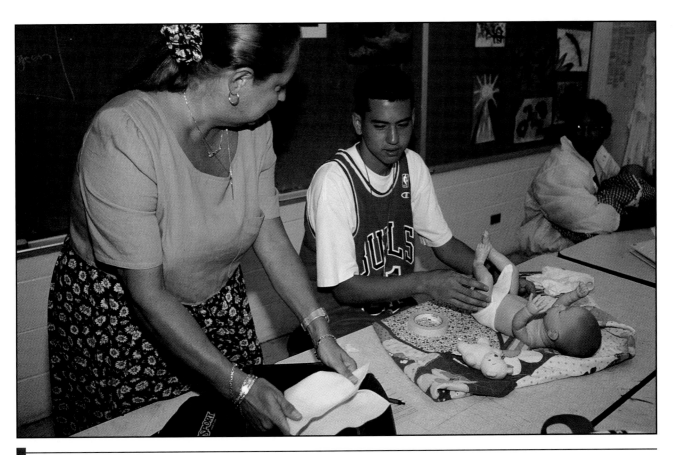

Marcy Reginelli, a teacher at Lutheran High School of Hawaii, Honolulu, demonstrates how to change a diaper. Student Ryan Scudder carefully follows each step. *(James A. Arendale)*

From left, first graders Sean Pi, Chad LaPointe and Nicole Pagnini, portraying sinners, try to find some way to be rid of their burden of sin during a chapel service at Ascension Lutheran School, Torrance, Calif. *(Carol Geisler)*

Ane Ertzner assembles large-print booklets for convalescent home patients and shut-ins at Our Savior, Cupertino, Calif. She makes the booklets from large-print Bible verses and illustrations in greeting cards. *(Earl Davidson)*

Basic dentistry is one way that a missionary team helps people in rural areas of Papua New Guinea. Dr. Lawrence, a native dentist with the team, fills cavities and extracts teeth during the expeditions. He provided the first dental clinic for the Hewa people in November 1994. *(Steve Lutz)*

Moving a health team into rural areas of Papua New Guinea takes thoughtful planning and plenty of muscle. At center is Dr. Steve Lutz, medical missionary. The medical project, supported by LCMS World Relief, provides health care to the Nate, Penale and Hewa people. *(Steve Lutz)*

Missionary Jo Treglown serves with her husband, Rev. Don Treglown, in the Philippines. Jo, right, and Perla mix skin ointment for a health worker seminar. *(Donald Treglown)*

Therefore, as we have opportunity,
let us do good to all people,
especially to those who belong
to the family of believers
(Gal. 6:10).

A woman of the Eleme people in Onne, located in Rivers State, Nigeria, prepares cassava. The Lutheran Church of Nigeria is an LCMS partner church. *(Barbara Ross)*

Previous page: Tami Waikin is a pharmacist at Immanuel Lutheran Hospital in Papua New Guinea. His colorful umbrella keeps away the rain as he accompanies the family of Missionary Lutz to Mt. Giluwe. *(Steve Lutz)*

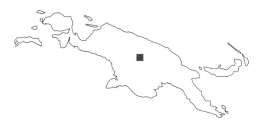

Marlene Jamrose volunteers her time for the local chapter of an international braille organization. A group of women at Trinity, Hammond, Ind., meets regularly to translate braille materials and assemble books. *(John Hassel)*

Get ready, set, go! Rev. William Geis of St. John, Lone Wolf, Okla., founded the "Jesus Club" for children, a place to go for fun activities after school. Today Vicar Randy Bard is in charge of the sack race. *(Willard G. Wegner)*

Lori Allen practices green-thumb stewardship of God's creation at her church, Woodlands, Montverde, Fla. *(Kent Swanson)*

Martin Tressler tills the preschool garden for spring planting at Good Shepherd, State College, Pa. *(M. H. Voth)*

Tyler Rank enjoys the playground at Faith, Merritt Island, Fla. *(Linda Lawrence)*

Greeting cards take shape as a colorful place mat, to be sold at an LWML fund-raiser. Toni Barnum of Faith, Merritt Island, Fla., displays the handiwork. *(Linda Lawrence)*

Wheels keep on rolling as kindergartners enjoy roller skating day at Trinity, Delray Beach, Fla. In the foreground are Lindsay Brandt, Mary Guelzow and Corinne Spies. *(Rebecca Miller)*

Sixth and seventh graders enjoy Christian fellowship during religion class at Concordia, Sarasota, Fla. From left, the students are Sarah Swerdfeger, Justin Patrizzi, David Rayburn, Danny Williams and Cynthia McElwee. *(Brenda Flegler)*

Susan Boerger's second grade class of Bethany Lutheran School, Parma, Ohio, holds Native American Day. She and student David Liese discuss a project. *(Marc Liese)*

Young artist Kailee Baird, a member of St. Paul, Denham, Ind., sculpts a clay masterpiece at her grandmother's house. *(Mildred Redweik)*

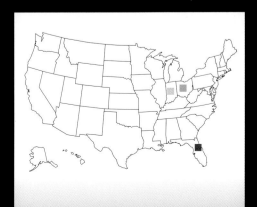

Only half of the choir made practice this week at Concordia, Wilmington, Del., but the smaller number didn't diminish Buddy's listening pleasure. *(Helene E. Schmidt)*

Garrett Robert Redweik and his great-grandmother, Antonia Arndt Gudas, enjoy a basket of flowers. Garrett's ancestors include more than 10 generations of Lutherans recorded in Lithuania. The family lives in Indiana. *(Mildred Redweik)*

Fashionable four-year-old Kourtnee Susan Baird models her Lithuanian great-grandmother's hat. *(Mildred Redweik)*

Volunteers Ted and Ann Vieweg, of Trinity, Hammond, Ind., pick up Meals on Wheels and prepare to deliver them. *(John Hassel)*

The Lutheran Association for Elementary Education of Fort Wayne, Ind., provides worship opportunities for its students, including a weekly all-school chapel service shown here at Emmanuel. *(Clair Winesburg)*

Rev. Karl R. Davies, pastor of Trinity, Hammond, Ind., visits Donald Weberus in his home and gives him Communion. *(John Hassel)*

Missionary Khurram Mehdi Khan works on teaching materials at the office of the People Of the Book Lutheran Outreach (POBLO), at St. Michael, Wayne, Mich. *(Russell H. Poulson)*

Bethanee Sunderman and Crystal Maxson strike up with the band of Trinity Lutheran School, Jackson, Mich. *(Connie Blackwood)*

Students from Trinity Lutheran School, Clinton Township, Mich., wear period costumes and practice a sea chantey before touring historical Greenfield Village, in Dearborn, Mich. *(David Tirsell)*

First graders at Trinity Lutheran School, Jackson, Mich., observe a demonstration by a paramedic on how to transport a victim. Pictured with the class are Jennifer Crooks, teacher; Craig Seppa, CEO of Jackson Emergency Medical Services and father of the student on the stretcher; and Wes Calkins, paramedic. *(Connie Blackwood)*

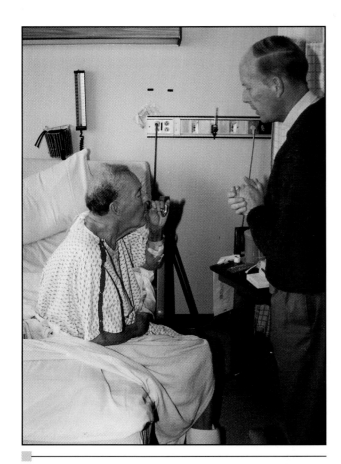

Our Lord is present with us everywhere—even in the hospital. Here, Pastor Jon Reusch, Cross of Christ, Bloomfield Hills, Mich., administers Communion to Ray Casey. *(James L. Fearing)*

As part of his work as a missionary to the Arab population of greater Detroit, Rev. Randy Duncan works on articles for the *Minaret*. His office is located at the People Of the Book Lutheran Outreach (POBLO), St. Michael, Wayne, Mich. *(Russell H. Poulson)*

It's more fun when we do things together! Nicholas Smurda watches Kameron Norton and Hannah Day go down the slide together at Zion School, Hinsdale, Ill. *(Ruta Jensen)*

The Thursday evening service at Immanuel, Freeport, Ill, is especially attractive to members with disabilities because of the less formal atmosphere. *(Lynn Hoefle)*

Ladies at Faith, Godfrey, Ill., support various social ministries with their quilting. *(Carol Kuhlmann)*

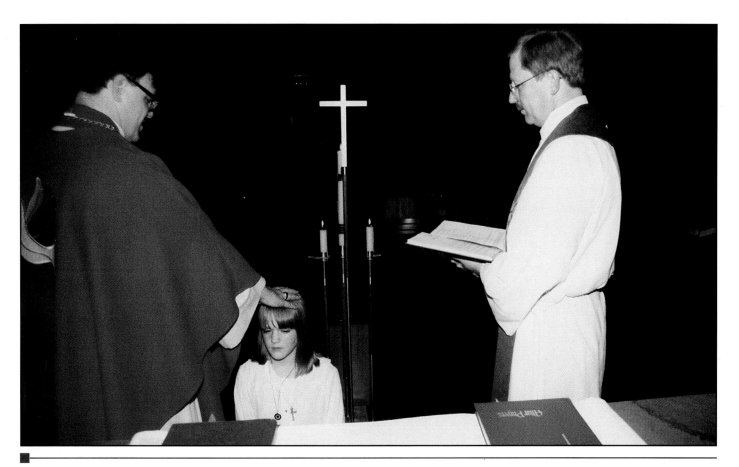

Pastors Stephen Wiest and Kenneth Widing of the campus ministry at the University of Wisconsin-Milwaukee and confirmand Eva Wiest. *(Robert B. Wendorf)*

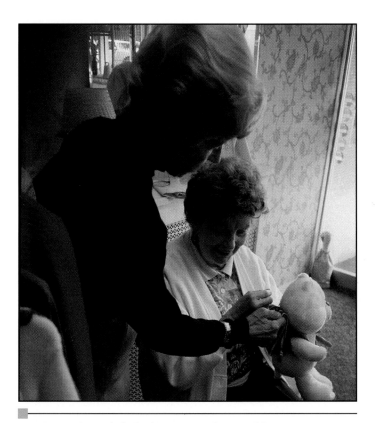

Loraine Walters, left, looks on as Dolores Schlessman sews a tag on a Rainbow Friends Doll for the Lutheran Child and Family Services Nice Twice Resale Shop, Mt. Vernon, Ill. The doll is given to each foster care child or adult and often becomes a surrogate parent or friend to discuss one's problems. *(Kent Smith)*

Barbara Pahl, Early Childhood Exceptional Needs Educational Assistant, works with Phillip Redman at Highlands School, Appleton, Wis. Both are members of Faith, Appleton. *(Glenn Ocock)*

Ninety-two-year-old Otto Geske, a member of First, Hot Springs, Ark., makes braille for Lutheran Braille Workers, Inc. at the church fellowship hall. Here he sorts the printing plates in preparation for pressing braille. *(Roy A. Jacob)*

Crystal Rodeman and Abigail Rees, students at Clemons Lutheran School, Clemons, Iowa, post signs to encourage fellow students to reach their goal: collect and recycle enough bottles and cans to raise $1,000 for a new multipurpose building. *(Bonnie Berrey)*

It's another typical day at work for the staff of the Southern District office, New Orleans, La. Here Joan Green, left, mailroom coordinator, and Marion Kennedy, assistant to the president, discuss an upcoming district-wide mailing. *(Marvin D. Otto)*

Music teacher Jack Flick gives violin lessons to third- and fourth-grade students at Zion Lutheran Academy, Fort Wayne, Ind. *(Eileen Porter)*

Every Thursday morning, these women from Mount Olive, Duluth, Minn., volunteer at St. Luke's Hospital and Trauma Center. Posing with puppets are, seated from left, Josephine Gauthier and Hertha Muehring; standing from left, Martha Aho, Viola Miller, Irene Possehl, Arlene Ruzich and Erna Gitar. *(David H. Duncan)*

A stone on the church steps at Zion, Palmyra, Mo., reminds members of their German roots. *(K. S. Gosney)*

Luverne police chief Keith Aanenson uses Safety Pup to teach safety to the children of the Little Lambs Preschool Nursery class at St. John, Luverne, Minn. Chief Aanenson is a member at St. John. *(Kristin Suhr)*

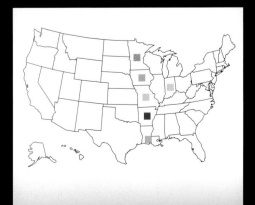

Mary Kae Christiansen, left, and Jessica Moennig pray during chapel service at Trinity, Freistatt, Mo. *(Fawn Hansen)*

This class of Ingrian pastors and deacons poses for a photograph at the end of a two-week in-service training program at the Lutheran Center in Moscow. The program is sponsored by the LCMS Board for Mission Services through the seminary of the Ingrian Lutheran Church in St. Petersburg, Russia.

Patty Crane, a member of Zion, Palmyra, Mo., arranges fruit at the C&R supermarket in Palmyra, where she is in charge of the produce department. *(K. S. Gosney)*

Loretta Urban, administrative assistant at St. Paul, New Melle, Mo., works in the church office. *(Jerry Snell)*

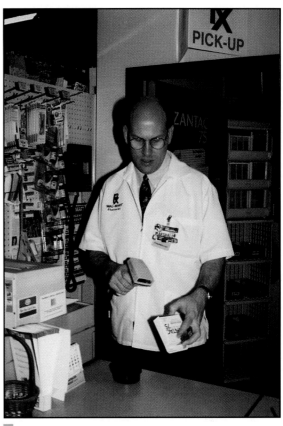

Wal-Mart pharmacy customers in Atchison, Kan., can always count on pharmacist Marshall Berry to be helpful and courteous. Berry is a member of Trinity, Atchison. *(Roschelle Bisping)*

Sisters in Christ: From left, Amanda Maass, Jessica Barnett, Emily Moffatt and Amanda Smith comprise the graduating eighth-grade class at St. John Lutheran School, Okarche, Okla. They have attended school together since childhood. Emily Moffatt and Amanda Smith are making their own "creation" of the "live long and prosper" sign from the "Star Trek" TV and movie series. *(Delinda Barnett)*

The preschool class at St. John, Okarche, Okla., puts on its walkin' shoes and sings about walkin' for Jesus during its spring program. *(Delinda Barnett)*

147

Gary Williams and Alex Jagger enjoy sitting in tires during the lunch hour at Grace Lutheran School, Arlington, Texas. *(Edward Naumann)*

Student Bill Sather leads a discussion of sound for the theater in stage-craft class in the Theater Arts Center at Concordia College, St. Paul, Minn. *(Timothy J. Bode)*

On "Take your daughter to work day" Kathy Digman, a teacher at the Gloria Dei Early Childhood Program, Houston, Texas, and her daughter, Kristina, show caterpillars to kindergartners Katelyn Norman and Christopher Burright. *(Betty J. Wagner)*

Happy and smiling, Ruth Breckenhauer braves the wind and captures her friend's hairnet on the St. Paul parking lot, West Point, Neb. *(Gwen Lindberg)*

148

The first freshman high school class at San Antonio Lutheran High School, 1995–96, on the property of Concordia School, San Antonio, Texas. Another grade will be added each year. *(Toni Hanes)*

It's lunch time at Sioux Falls Lutheran School, S.D., and Annette Leggett uses the computer during her free time. *(Lynda Strobel)*

Chaplain Steve Lee and Officer Travis Thiede of the Colorado Springs, Colo., Police Department. Officer Thiede has just had a vehicle towed in and is completing paperwork. *(Steve Lee)*

Emily Rose Brandt of Loveland, Colo., learns to skate. She is a member of Immanuel, Loveland. *(Lani Rose Brandt)*

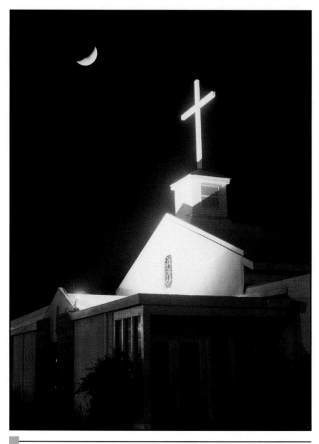

The cross on St. James, Imperial Beach, Calif., shines in the darkness reminding us that Christ is the Light of the World. *(John C. Rumsey III)*

Matie Rollert is tying one of the many quilts made by the Redeemer, Thousand Oaks, Calif., sewing group. *(Theodore R. Dibble)*

Jennifer Stewart wishes her dog, Trisha, a good morning. Jennifer belongs to Christ, LaMesa, Calif. *(Jane Thompson)*

Lisa Gerlach hands out worship folders at Zion, Anaheim, Calif. *(Sandie Tufts)*

151

Victor Tognazinni examines mold growing on strawberries in a field in Santa Maria, Calif. Victor is a member of Our Savior, Santa Maria. *(Wayne Taylor)*

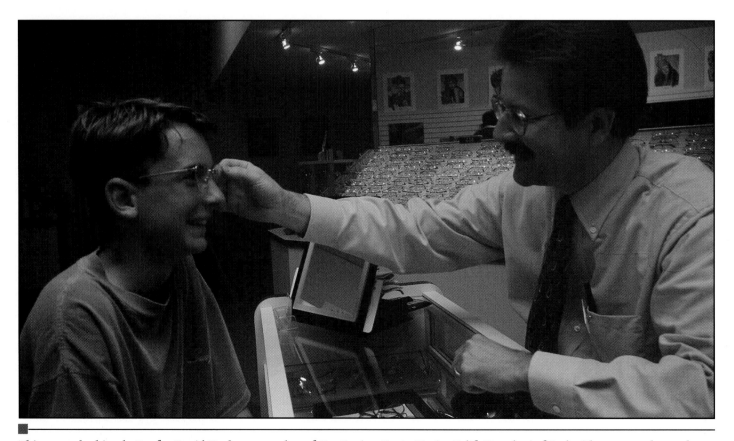

Things are looking better for David Taylor, a member of Our Savior, Santa Maria, Calif. Here he is fitted with new eyeglasses by optometrist John Prewitt. *(Wayne Taylor)*

Pilot Ardis Edwards is ready for take-off at the Livermore, Calif., airport. Edwards is a member of Our Savior, Fremont, Calif. *(Ardis Edwards)*

A weekly occurrence: Bill Fletcher, a member of First, Hot Springs, Ark., prepares breakfast in the church kitchen for the Wednesday morning men's Bible class. *(Roy A. Jacob)*

153

During chapel service, Pastor Michael Ramming, Grace, Killeen, Texas, shares the Question Box with students of Grace Lutheran School. *(Tim Matthys)*

Choir director Rebecca Frandsen and pianist Jim Martinez take a well-deserved break during rehearsal at Redeemer, Thousand Oaks, Calif. *(Theodore R. Dibble)*

After a long day in class, second graders from Bethany Lutheran School, Long Beach, Calif., do what they do best at recess—horse around. *(Felix Rivera)*

It may be off-Broadway, but these children of Christ, LaMesa, Calif., dance and sing up a storm during rehearsal for the school musical. *(Jane Thompson)*

Polly Hogan is affectionately known as the "banner lady" at Bethel, San Francisco, Calif. Polly's artistic talents have contributed much to the worship life of her congregation. *(Kathie Badertscher)*

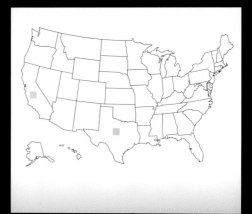

155

Listeners participate by calling in to this Bible study on the air. At KFUO radio, the Synod's radio station in St. Louis, Rev. Todd Wilken, left, serves as guest leader. He is pastor of Holy Cross, Sugar Loaf Township, Ill. Program producer Steve Lewis is in the center (behind window) and Chuck Rathert, right, serves as host for the program. *(Paul Ockrassa)*

The Food Closet volunteers of Prince of Peace, Tacoma, Wash., surprised Jim Lauer with a special cake for his 76th birthday. *(John Schmidt)*

Pam Larson's preschool students enjoy learning about teamwork by performing a parachute activity at Beautiful Savior, Spokane, Wash. *(Charles Brondos)*

Rev. Michael Kasting, the "dinner dean" for the supper hour of the LOGOS Midweek School at Faith, Sequim, Wash., blows the ram's horn to call students to order. The pastor is wearing a Khoufieh as part of the evening's theme "A Trip to Israel." *(Paul Honore)*

Someone will be warmer this winter because Evelyn Harris, Trinity, Bellingham, Wash., makes quilts for the Lighthouse Mission. *(Carl Sahlhoff)*

Church secretary Eggy Lorenzo makes sure that there's a place for everything and everything is in its place at Our Savior, Aiea, Hawaii. *(James Arendale)*

Ralph Springer at Faith, East Wenatchee, Wash., demonstrates how his father and grandfather used to sit in an old rocker and read the Bible. *(Shirley Porter)*

157

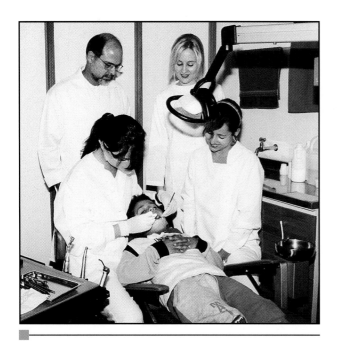

Barrio children in Esteio, Brazil, plant a vegetable garden as part of the education program of Villa Pedreira Mission Center.

A team provides dental care for children who attend classes at the Villa Pedreira Mission Center in Esteio, Brazil. The center, supported by donors to LCMS World Relief, provides formal and informal education for 160 children.

In Esteio, Brazil, children play outside "Amigo dos meninos"—Portuguese for Friend of Street Children—a residential home where they receive schooling, food and training in a safe, caring place.

Children in the Esteio barrio dramatize the resurrection story in the mission center. In a community that is being transformed with assistance from outside resources, the school gives hope for the children's future, including new life in Christ.

School children learn to bake at the Residential Home and Vocational School for Street Children in Esteio, Brazil. Once abandoned to the streets, the youngsters are attending school and learning trades, thanks to donations from Missouri Synod Lutherans through LCMS World Relief.

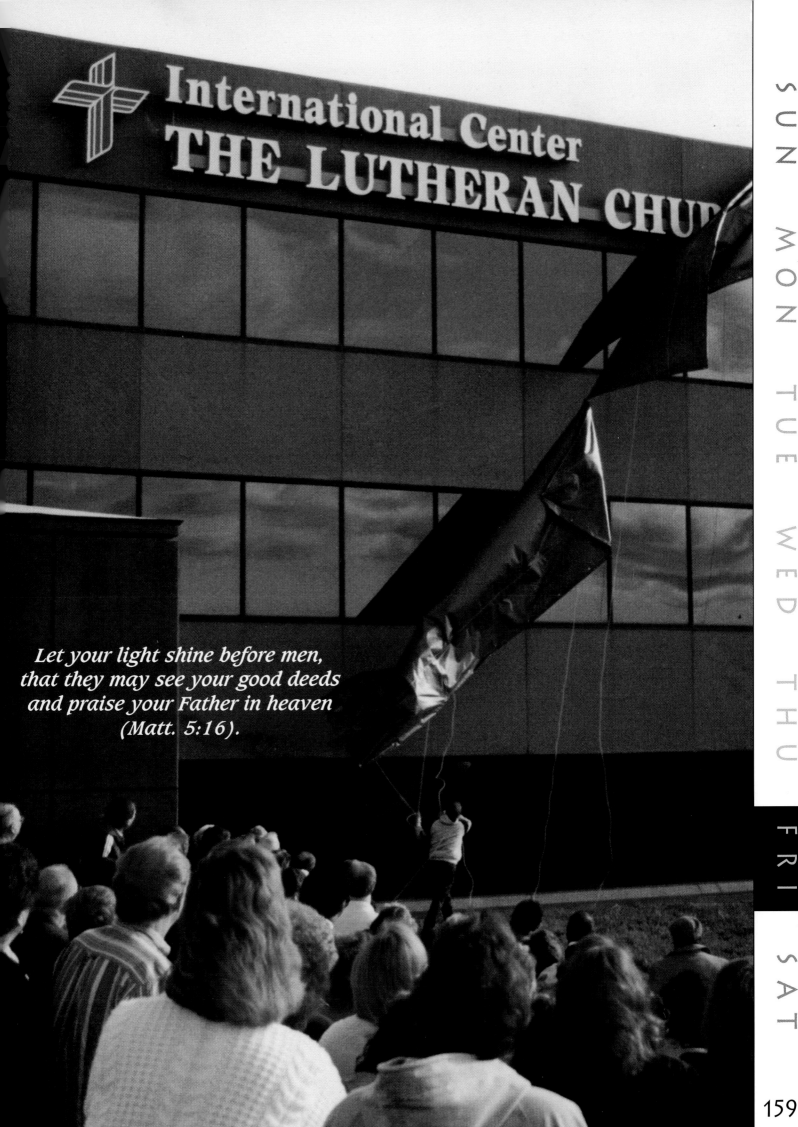

Let your light shine before men, that they may see your good deeds and praise your Father in heaven (Matt. 5:16).

At Good Shepherd, Saginaw, Mich., Ellen Pritzlaff gets groceries ready for delivery to the city rescue mission. *(Eugene D. Mossner)*

Mary Overdorff plays ball outside Luther Haven Retirement Community in Oviedo, Fla. *(John Gaudette)*

Isabelle Gallandt, St. John, Pinconning, Mich., bursts with surprise when she discovers there is a 50th anniversary party for her and her husband, Richard. *(Ron Wetters)*

Previous page: Staff witness the unveiling of a new, lighted sign on the exterior of the Synod's International Center in St. Louis, Mo. *(Suzanne Johnson)*

Isabelle and Richard Gallandt link arms as their friends dance around them in St. John's fellowship hall, Pinconning, Mich. *(Ron Wetters)*

Nurse Mary Niemeyer, Martini Church, Baltimore, Md., cares for John Shanley in her home and takes him for a stroll in Federal Hill Park. *(Mary Lynn Biggs)*

Martin Lotz Jr., St. Paul, Kingsville, Md., groans, "I can't believe he hit that!" *(Timothy J. Caslow)*

Preschoolers from Faith, Merritt Island, Fla., enjoy playing outside. From left, are Amanda Parker, Jamie Waldron, Amanda Starnes, Lauren Barber, Miles Kincaid and Jonathan Brown. *(Linda Lawrence)*

Our Little Lambs Daycare and Preschool of Faith, Merritt Island, Fla., holds its own Olympics. *(Linda Lawrence)*

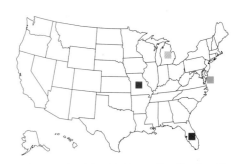

Volunteer George Havens carries out laundry detail at Advent House, a hospice-care home, an outreach of Perinton Ecumenical Ministries Inc. Advent House is located next to Risen Christ, Fairport, N.Y. *(Frank E. Grant)*

Pastor Gene Rehwinkel of Concordia, Sarasota, Fla., explains baptism to Caroline Elizabeth Hecht, 22 months, as he gives her a close-up view of the baptismal font at St. Paul, Falls Church, Va.

Studying the Word: Erick and Sharon Koehling, members of Redeemer, Richland, Wash., host their church's Couples Club that meets for Bible study and prayer. *(Walt Wendland)*

Pouring concrete on a Laborers For Christ project at St. Matthew, Lee's Summit, Mo. *(Eugene L. Amen)*

Richard Kaiser, Our Savior, Glennie, Mich., splits wood at his home. *(Marie Kaiser)*

Kathy Zontek, Student Council supervisor, and students Amy Spring and Cassandra Schanne sell popcorn at Trinity Lutheran School, Jackson, Mich. This is a monthly activity to support David Erber, a missionary in Nigeria. *(Connie Blackwood)*

"Praise Him with the sounding of the trumpet" (Psalm 150:3). The trumpets and clarinets of St. Lorenz School, Frankenmuth, Mich., join the rest of the band in a concert. *(William G. Rummal)*

The circus has come to St. Mark Lutheran Preschool, Brunswick, Ohio. Abigail Wolfe and Heather Cesareo join the other "prancing ponies" as part of the circus parade. *(George C. Yanda)*

Sunday's service will be brighter for the members of Trinity, Hammond, Ind., thanks to Bill Ball, custodian. *(John H. Hassel)*

Crossing guard Betony Cose greets kindergartner Whitney Peterson as she arrivies for school at St. Paul, Stevens Point, Wis. *(Randy Lindemann)*

Chaplain Vernon Bettermann, right, and three of his parishioners from St. Peter, East Peoria, Ill., inspect a new aircraft for the 182nd Airlift Wing, of which they are all members. From left, Steve Thomas, Kim Thomas and Roger Maiters. The 182nd Airlift Wing is part of the Illinois Air National Guard. *(Thomas Buzzell)*

Five couples of Ascension, East Peoria, Ill., meet for Bible study every other Friday evening. This evening Laurel and Sharon Peterson serve as hosts in their Germantown Hills home. Other couples involved are Chuck and Phyllis Wiechmann, Stan and Arlene Rush, Dick and Sandy Linse, and Anita and Al Knack. *(Al Knack)*

The blessing and dedication of Camp Wartburg, Waterloo, Ill., after being taken over by Lutheran Child and Family Services of Illinois. Officers discussing future plans are Gene Svebakken, Rev. Herbert Mueller, Linda Glaenzer, Al Frost, Gary Buatte, Dorothy Mansholt and B. J. Chakiris. *(Jane Lucht)*

Rev. George Gude, Emmaus, Dorsey, Ill., first vice president of the Southern Illinois District, left, and Rev. Herbert Mueller, president of the Southern Illinois District, discuss business at a district board of directors meeting. *(Jane Lucht)*

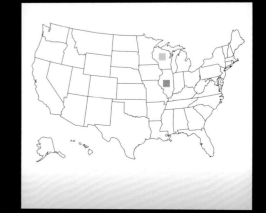

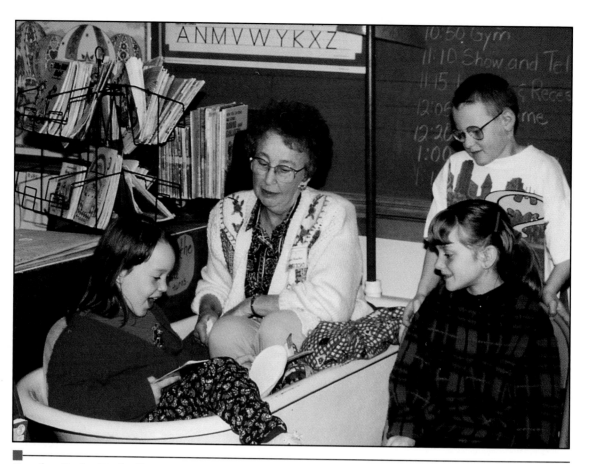

Grandma Janice Kuehn listens intently as Amanda Schmidt reads her a "bathtub" story on Grandparents Day, St. Paul School, Bonduel, Wis. *(Curt Schneider)*

U.S. Senator Conrad Burns from Montana meets with William Hecht, right, St. Paul, Falls Church, Va. Hecht represents a number of organizations including the Boy Scouts in Washington D.C.

Jacob Scott and Cody Meister checked the gopher trap, and they got one! St. Paul-Artesian, Waverly, Iowa. *(Kathleen Scott)*

Aaron Likens, 13, carries the crucifix to lead the procession exiting the International Center Chapel. The worshipers are going outside for the unveiling of a new lighted sign outside the building. *(Suzanne Johnson)*

Rev. Paul Devantier, executive director of the Synod's Board for Communication Services, speaks at the dedication of a new sign at the Synod's International Center. In back, are Synod President A. L. Barry, left, and Missouri District President James W. Kalthoff, right. *(Suzanne Johnson)*

Debbie Klinge, Our Redeemer, Dubuque, Iowa, home schools her son, Daniel, at their kitchen table, as she does for all five of her children. *(Ann K. Scott)*

Dorothy and Jean Lou McGregor, members of Our Savior, Glennie, Mich., chop a hole in the ice so their cattle can have fresh water. *(Marie Kaiser)*

Andrew Beeks and Katie Hathaway raise the U.S. flag outside their school, St. Paul, Fort Wayne, Ind. *(Clair Winesburg)*

Every week Bruno Daube, center, a member at Trinity, Lombard, Ill., visits Lakeview nursing home. Here, Virginia Vernon, right, shows Daube and resident Leonard Purim how she danced the Flamenco when she was young in Spain. *(Bill Cooper)*

Workers erect the steel girders for the new sanctuary of Immanuel, Memphis, Tenn. The LCEF-funded building will be dedicated Nov. 24, 1996. *(Ronald Wiese)*

Debbie Lowry, St. John, Emporia, Va., lends a hand in the construction of an addition to her church. The project is being aided by Laborers For Christ. *(George Plvan)*

Fifth-grader Vikki Varga studies her science lesson at Bethany Lutheran School, Parma, Ohio. *(Marc Liese)*

The Crader family, members at Faith, Godfrey, Ill., gather together for family devotions. *(Carol Kuhlmann)*

Second-grade "construction workers" singing in the "Oh Me, Oh My, Nehemiah" first–third grade program at Central Luthern School, St. Paul, Minn. From left are Mallery Boeyink, Jessica Wilson, Travis Schulze, Joanna Vinz, Sandra James, John Stage and Susan Fohrenkamm. *(Jerry Gabrielson)*

A student at St. John Lutheran School, Ellisville, Mo., decorates a vase for his Mother's Day gift. *(Paula Schlueter Ross)*

The McFarlands, Bruce and Karen (choir director), lead the singing at the St. Paul, St. Joseph, Mo., Happy Campers Camp Out at Big Lake State Park. *(Greg Beechner)*

Jennifer Mattson of St. Paul, St. Joseph, Mo., keeps an eye on the family dog, who assumes she also is invited for dinner. *(Greg Beechner)*

Tom Willenborg, Trinity, Baton Rouge, La., is manager at the Macaroni Grill. Here he flames a sauteed pasta dish. *(Beverly A. Huxsoll)*

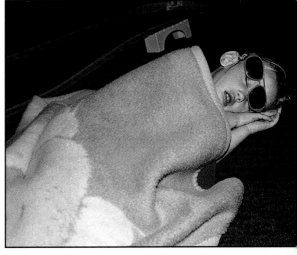

Emily Rolf, 3, just couldn't stay awake any longer. So Grandma Joyce Schiroo, First, Glencoe, Minn., covered her with a blanket. *(Ken Schiroo)*

Children are instructed in craft activities at a "Parents' Night Out" event sponsored by St. Paul, Sedalia, Mo. *(Dennis Hall)*

173

Lutheran Hour speakers Dr. Dale Meyer, left, and Dr. Wallace Schulz in a recording studio at the headquarters of the International Lutheran Laymen's League, St. Louis, Mo. *(Dave Kuenzel)*

Thea Ferge, a member of St. Paul, Artesian, Waverly, Iowa, and baby John Scott greet a resident of the Denver (Iowa) Sunset Home, where Thea is the activity coordinator. *(Kathleen Scott)*

With a melody in her heart, Janet Goll, First Lutheran, Ponca City, Okla., practices handbells. *(Garth Hannum)*

Longtime deacon and elder John Lewis is laid to rest from St. Paul, Ashland, Ky. "Heav'n's morning breaks, and earth's vain shadows flee; In life, in death, O Lord, abide with me." *(Mary H. Robinson)*

Overhauling the motor of a large air compressor is easy for Bill Detmer, employee of Quartzite Stone Co., Lincoln County, Kan. He is a member of St. John, Lincoln, Kan. *(Ken Greene)*

At St. John, Ellisville, Mo., scoutmasters Mark Moyer, sitting, and Larry Hellwig make plans with scouts, from left, R. J. Hunter, Steve Hellwig, Kyle Erdbruegger and Mike Puricelli. *(Dave Kuenzel)*

Kindergartner Ashley Payne pushes Chelsea McCullough (prekindergarten student) at First Lutheran School, Ponca City, Okla. *(Garth Hannum)*

Teacher Karl Bergdolt "enjoys" a pie-in-the-face from Jana Bates at the Trinity, Grand Island, Neb., school carnival. *(Oscar Bredthauer Jr.)*

Lutheran coronation float in the Battle of Flowers parade in San Antonio, Texas. Pictured are, front to back, Meagan Knippa, Lindsay Lange, Sarah Rose Schneider, and reigning queen Kelly Paige Sewell. *(Toni Hanes)*

What a pyramid! The fifth and sixth graders in tumbling class at St. Paul, Perham, Minn. *(John Gottschalk)*

Michelle Whiting enjoys a beautiful spring day on the playground at First Lutheran School, Ponca City, Okla. *(Garth Hannum)*

Chaplain Edward Kletzien walks with WW II veteran Robert Kraeplin at the Wisconsin Veterans Home in King, Wis. The North Wisconsin District supports Chaplain Kletzien's ministry at the home. *(Glenn Ocock)*

Jayne Uelner, Our Redeemer, Dubuque, Iowa., home schooling her two children, Nathan and Ashley. *(Ann K. Scott)*

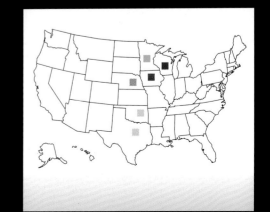

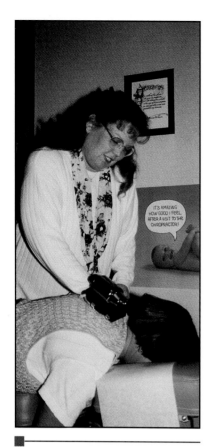

Dr. Jeane Koenen of Trinity, Atchison, Kan., gives a treatment to Vickie Scholz, receptionist and patient, at the Koenen Chiropractic Clinic. *(Roschelle Bisping)*

Eric Pankonien, Kendra Haseloff, Chris Stangeland, Lisa Gunter, Angela Stangeland and Eric Henriksen in devotion at Peace, Garland, Texas. *(Randy Vonderheid)*

Retirees Elton Striker, Robert Schrup and Pat Fisher, members of St. John, Burwell, Neb., test their fishing skills at Calamus Lake. Although much of the work has been passed to the next generation, these supportive men remain a vital part of it all. *(Sue Switzer)*

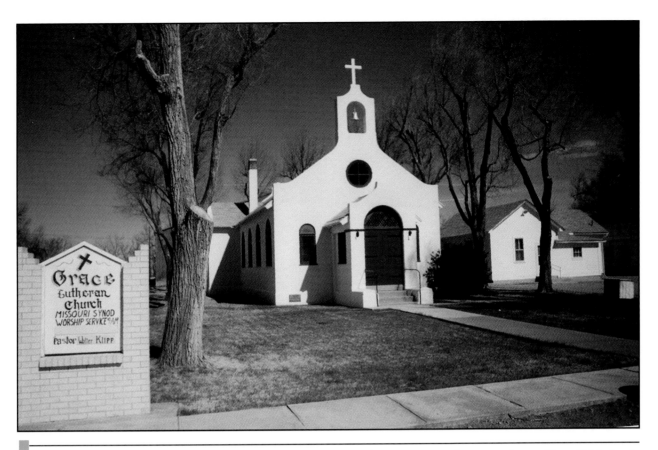

Times change. Grace, Sugar City, Colo., established in 1937, now has 24 communicant members. *(Donald Markus)*

Micah Maly and other first graders learn hand signals at Immanuel, Loveland, Colo. *(Lani Rose Brandt)*

Paula's Plants, a wholesale greenhouse, is the family business of Alan and Paula Schneider and son Chris, members of Zion, New Salem, N.D. *(Peg Reuther)*

Justin Crews, a member of Trinity, Bellingham, Wash., shows off "Tilly," his entry at the Whatcom County Youth Fair. (Tilly is a Mille Fleur chicken.) The event took place at the Lynden Fair Grounds in Lynden, Wash. *(Carl Sahlhoff)*

Elfie Wetzstein adds the heavenly sounds of the harp to parish events at Bethlehem, Carson City, Nev. *(John Gamble)*

President A. L. Barry shares a story during a morning meeting with his staff. Left, is assistant Paul McCain; right, assistant Ken Schurb and secretary Brenda Schreder. *(Suzanne Johnson)*

Diane Linsdau, left, and Karen Rumsey prepare pizza for a fund-raiser at St. James, Imperial Beach, Calif. *(John C. Rumsey III)*

Thank You, Lord! Travis Clifford prays with intensity over lunch in Tomball, Texas. Travis is a member of St. John, Cypress, Texas. *(Judy Scattergood)*

Jesus Ochoa, right, a member of Redeemer Saturday School, Atascadero, Calif., prepares for a Special Olympics parade in Morro Bay, Calif. *(Bonnie Pixley)*

18

Second and third graders at Bethany Lutheran School, Long Beach, Calif., wonder what could be better than a cool popsicle on a hot afternoon. *(Felix Rivera)*

Captain Carl R. Rau, chaplain at Fort Lewis, Wash., welcomes Chuck and Lori Knowles who are seeking counsel. *(John Schmidt)*

Bryan Lindemood, an elementary education major at Concordia University, River Forest, Ill., plays with one of the 150 children from the community who come to the Early Childhood Center on Concordia's campus. *(Kristin A. Walsh)*

182

Ashley Aylett and Rebekah Schmidt share their friendship at a birthday party at Gig Harbor, Wash.
(John Schmidt)

Father Fitz puts a "cross hat" on Meredith Rix at Community Lutheran, Escondido, Calif., to remind us of God's best gift, salvation in Jesus Christ. *(Rebecca E. Schoepp)*

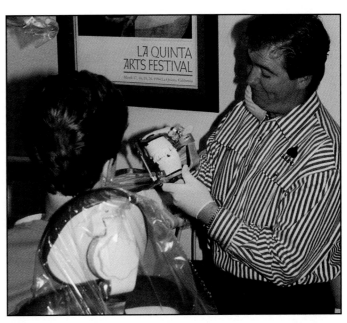

One member serving another: Dr. Blake Mueller gives dental treatment to Janet Dibble. Both are members at Redeemer, Thousand Oaks, Calif. *(Theodore R. Dibble)*

183

Teaching remains an important responsibility for missionaries and their families. In Dapaon, Togo (West Africa), Stephanie Schulte and Dambé Laré teach a class for children.

In Wuhan, China, students pause for mealtime at the South Central Seminary. The Synod does not have missionaries in China, but assists with printing of Bibles, provides exchange faculty and some educational materials for seminaries.

Dambé Laré, left, holds one of the books used for children's classes in Dapaon, Togo. From left, are Laré, Jeffrey Schulte, Thomas Schulte, Mangle Tilate, Yielig, Timothy Schulte, Yendukoi, Poying, Tchschov-tchshou and Ariana Schulte. The Schultes are children of Gary and Stephanie Schulte, missionaries in Dapaon.

A Christian distributes wall posters outside a rural church in Miaoling, China.

*I can do everything
through Him [Christ]
who gives me strength
(Phil. 4:13).*

At the Miango Rest Home in Nigeria, children from missionary families visit with the children of the president of the Lutheran Church of Nigeria during a break in their vacation Bible school. Front row, from left, Luke Erber, Amaowo Udofia; middle row, Joshua Udofia, Phillip New; back row, Liza Udofia, Victoria New, Jonathon Erber. *(Barbara Ross)*

More than 50 members of St. Paul, N. Tonawanda, N.Y., participated in a chowder/baked goods sale to benefit a financially stricken family. Over $2,000 was raised including matching funds from AAL. *(Dennis Demmin)*

Previous page: Patricia Northrup knows there is time for both softball and studying at Concordia College, Bronxville, N.Y. *(John Warner)*

Members of Christ Memorial, Malvern, Pa., participate in a benefit crafts show. Irene McFadden is shown here inspecting her plaques of Bible verses and pressed flowers. *(Edgar Buerger)*

The wedding begins soon: Marilyn Leland, soon to be a mother-in-law, talks with bride Holly Hoffmann prior to the wedding at St. Michael, Fort Meyers, Fla. *(Rita A. Waldren)*

Paul Rikkonen assembles playground equipment for the preschool at Immanuel, Manchester, N.H. *(Doug Gootee)*

Dewitt Gorman, Our Savior, Centereach, N.Y., shares the Gospel with an inmate at a nearby prison. *(Brian Garnier)*

Everyone takes a coffee break. Chaplain Ernest Knoche offers refills to Chaplain Christian Dahlberg and Specialist First Class Pamela Thomure at Regional Support Command in Oakdale, Pa. *(Jessica Knoche)*

The fourth and fifth graders at Concordia Lutheran School in Sarasota, Fla., get a new computer installed by resident volunteer expert Charles Scott. *(Brenda Flegler)*

This display, which summarizes the work of Martin Luther, won first prize at the Maryland State History Fair. The project designers are, from left, Nader Hawit, Travis Weiss and Andrew Kassouf, members of First Lutheran Church, Sunderland, Md. *(John Kassouf)*

Melanie Moore and Steven Lawrence seek the Lord's blessing as they join their lives together in holy matrimony at Good Shepherd, Shalimar, Fla. *(Bea Daily)*

Whether you call it "Brother John" or "Frère Jacques," the GLEAM members at Martin Luther Christian School in Pennsauken, N.J., could sing it in English, French, Spanish and Vietnamese thanks to their teacher, Tu Nguyen. *(Kenneth Wunsch)*

Van Tran watches intently as GLEAM members at Martin Luther Christian School in Pennsauken, N.J., join together for fun, fellowship and learning. *(Kenneth Wunsch)*

The McKinney family gets a bang out of life during a black powder shoot camp at Rendezvous. The McKinneys are members of Holy Cross, Eureka, Mont. *(Richard W. Payton)*

Three generations of LWMLers introduce the League to members of the up-and-coming fourth generation at the LWML zone rally at Grace, Fort Lauderdale, Fla. Pictured are Janet Sherrill, Debra Ryan, Velma Gunter, Allison Ryan and Emily Ryan. *(Marsha L. Holm)*

At the LWML zone rally at Grace, Fort Lauderdale, Fla., Bob Sherrill, Rev. George Earhart and Bill Russell entertain the ladies before lunch. *(Marsha L. Holm)*

Thomas Davison, Chris Bohne and Mark Palmer clear land for a beach volleyball court at Oak Road, Lilburn, Ga. *(Carl Horst)*

Ingham County, Mich., sponsors a Christmas in April program, where neighbors help neighbors in need. Here, Frank Malott and Walter Holz lend a helping hand, saw and drill to build a porch. Frank and Walter are members of St. Luke, Haslett. *(Walter L. Holz)*

Scott Hazel and Jessica Fricke assist Tommy Campo (on horse) at the closing ceremonies of the Woodlands Lutheran Ministries' Horses for the Handicapped event, Montverde, Fla. *(Kent Swanson)*

191

Members from Mount Calvary, Fort Wayne, Ind., clear trees from the land where their new church will be built. *(Paul W. Doenges)*

Rev. David Luecke leads a group in prayer at Community of Hope, Brecksville, Ohio. *(Deborah Phillips)*

Ruth Matty and her daughter, Rachel, members at Zion, Akron, Ohio, share a quiet moment at their home in Cuyahoga Falls. *(Christine McCune)*

Larry Faulkner and Steve Berning assemble new playground equipment for their preschool at Zion, Garrett, Ind. *(Julie Faulkner)*

Rhiannon Forrester, left, and Sara Wiehe dance at the 50s/60s sock hop held in the gym at Zion, Columbia City, Ind. *(Barbara Knuth)*

Fifth and sixth graders from Lutheran elementary schools compete in the St. Paul Lutheran Invitational Track Meet, held at the Ypsilanti High School, Ypsilanti, Mich. *(Connie Blackwood)*

193

After a heavy rain, Sarah Berning helps remove water from a playground under construction at Zion, Garrett, Ind. *(Julie Faulkner)*

This weekend finds Jerry Pankow serving others by building houses with Habitat for Humanity in Slidell, La. *(Emelda Remond)*

As part of the ministry of the People of the Book Lutheran Outreach (POBLO), Jenny Duncan, standing, and Cynthia Mehdi Khan, seated at right, share Bible stories with Pakistani children at Faith, Troy, Mich. *(Russell H. Poulson)*

For most teenagers, their 16th birthday means a driver's license. But for Tony Likes, Golden, Ill., it meant his first solo flight. Tony saved money from his paper route to pay for his flight lessons. He is at the Quincy, Ill., airport a few days after his first solo flight, getting ready for another. *(Roger Buss)*

Showing the way: Trustee Maurice Summerall and Pastor Linsey Dettmer erect a new sign that shows the way to their new mission church in Pigeon Forge, Tenn. *(Thelma Gooding)*

The youth room at Zion, Hinsdale, Ill., has a new coat of paint—and so do Julie Longerman, Emily Jensen and Erin Carlsen! The three helped paint Bible verses on the walls as a constant reminder of the beauty of God's Word. *(Ruta Jensen)*

God provides a new generation of pastors. South Wisconsin District President Ronald E. Meyer installs his son, Jeffrey, as associate pastor of First Immanuel, Cedarburg, Wis. *(Ronald Meyer)*

Modern parenting makes for creative church workers. Dad is elder on duty, so Mom, Julie Zimmer, plays flute as she rocks her son, Erik, to the beat of the music. Lloyd Liese adds the organ accompaniment at Trinity, Lombard, Ill. *(Bill Cooper)*

The clown team, Joyce Hawkins and Brian Anderson of Shepherd of the Grove, Maple Grove, Minn., brings the love of Christ to Marcella McLaughlin and the other residents of the Berkshire Nursing Home. *(John T. Roles)*

Leftovers from an estate sale are carried into the Our Savior Thrift Shop by members of Our Savior, Chicago, Ill. From left are Vera Andersen, Betty Yost, Patti Foerster and Oscar Andersen. *(Rosalie Streng)*

Pastor Henry Buchholz prepares for his message at the 5 p.m. Saturday worship service at St. Paul, Perham, Minn. *(Cleone Stewart)*

A precious moment at mealtime is a gentle reminder of the priceless gift of life granted by our heavenly Father. From left, Olivia, Tammy and Woodrow Nelson, and Jennifer Selle from St. John, Tigerton, Wis. *(Cindy Mueller)*

At Grandpa's woodworking shop Wesley Foster helps his grandson Jacob Scott with a special project. St. Paul, Artesian, Waverly, Iowa. *(Kathleen Scott)*

Sitting on a rock is a fine way to enjoy nature at Heit's Point Lutheran Camp, say Brett and Ryan Hall, members of St. Paul, Sedalia, Mo. *(Dennis Hall)*

Pat Schmid checks the meatballs prior to catering a banquet for Ducks Unlimited at the Tower Civic Center, Tower, Minn. Pat is a member of Gloria Dei, Virginia, Minn. *(Annette Herring)*

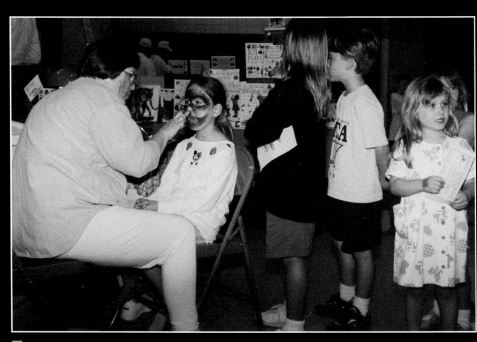

Children stand in line to have their faces painted by Barbara Mauldin at Trinity, Baton Rouge, La. The event was Family Fun Day, sponsored by the Parent-Teacher League of Baton Rouge Lutheran School. All proceeds go to the school for the purchase of non-budgeted items. *(Beverly A. Huxsoll)*

In the spirit of an old-fashioned barn raising, members of Trinity, Baton Rouge, La., construct a storage shed on the church grounds. From left, George Bruick, Don Bleviar, Eric Goodman, Carl Spaulding, Dean Dows. *(Beverly A. Huxsoll)*

Highway angel Paul Shropa prepares to attend the annual "Rolling Thunder Ride for Freedom," which honors Vietnam veterans. When not riding on his motorcycle, he can be found serving as pastor of Shepherd of the Grove, Maple Grove, Minn. *(John T. Roles)*

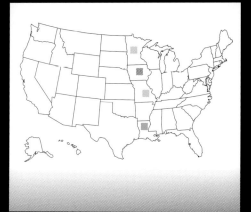

All aboard for the Passion Play! Senior citizens from St. Paul and St. John, Perham, Minn., are ready to board a bus to the Twin Cities to see a re-enactment of our Lord's Passion. *(Cleone Stewart)*

From left, Viola Heil, Helen Schweder and Marc Schweder plant flowers and soybeans in a planter in downtown Norborne, Mo. The group is getting ready for the 14th annual Soybean Festival, which will be held in August. A member of Trinity, Norborne, Marc has been the festival chairman for the past 13 years. *(Robert A. Raasch)*

Kirsten Nelson and Chris Pruitt begin their new life together as wife and husband at Ascension, Wichita, Kan. *(Ken White)*

A dirty job is more fun when you do it with friends. Members of Trinity, Garden City, Kan., serve the community by keeping the roadside clean. *(Bill Proctor)*

Jana Mayo, a member of Grace in Killeen, Texas, helps to keep their youth group portable building clean. *(Tim Matthys)*

Rev. Roberto Rojas uses the airwaves to spread the Gospel to Spanish-speaking people in and around Grand Island, Neb. He is seen here broadcasting from the studio of radio station KMMJ. *(Oscar Bredthauer Jr.)*

'I rejoiced" with those who said to me, 'Let us go to the house of the LORD' " (Psalm 122:1). With the cross still draped from Easter, the chancel of Grace, Killeen, Texas, welcomes people to worship. *(Tim Matthys)*

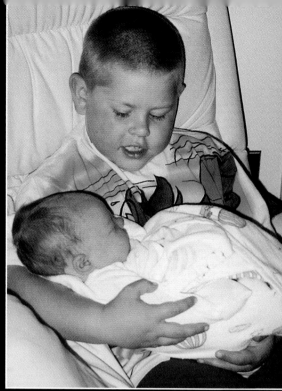

Big brother Jared Hashberger welcomes newborn sister Tiffany at St. Francis Memorial Hospital, West Point, Neb. Soon Tiffany will be welcomed into the family of God in baptism at St. Paul, West Point. *(Gwen Lindberg)*

Highway 30 east of Grand Island, Neb., is neat and clean thanks to Scott Smith, Andrew Carretto, Paul Saville and Brent Karsten,

Ted Price and Chris Schatzman check and measure their work against the blueprints. Members of Immanuel, Santa Fe, N.M., the two are helping to build a house for a Habitat for Humanity project in Santa Fe. *(Fred Rick)*

Kevan Cox of St. John, Okarche, Okla., prepares for his turn at bat during Okarche's annual Baseball Day activities. *(Delinda Barnett)*

The Mother/Daughter spring luncheon at Our Savior, Aracadia, Calif: the men, husbands and sons, are serving. *(Rick Krach)*

Leroy Hohle leads an outdoor worship service at the GT Ranch, Hockley, Texas. *(Ken Garrick)*

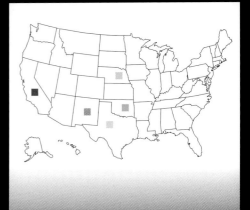

Members from Our Savior, Billings, Mont., join those of other area congregations in Billings to complete a Habitat for Humanity construction project. *(Gary A. Ostermiller)*

Seventh- and eighth-grade girls prepare dessert at a Western-theme school-dinner project at Immanuel, Loveland, Colo. *(Lani Rose Brandt)*

Eighty-five-year-old Senior Olympics champion L. K. "Sandy" Sandoval, right, of Immanuel, Santa Fe, N.M., practices his basketball skills with Pastor Douglas Escue. *(Fred Rick)*

Puget Sound Lutheran youth solicited a canned-food donation for the needy as part of the admission price to attend the dance sponsored by Good Shepherd, Tacoma, Wash., at Concordia Lutheran School. *(John Schmidt)*

Jared Wilkinson and Maithili Johnson of Concordia School enjoy the dance sponsored by Good Shepherd, Tacoma, Wash. *(John Schmidt)*

In her 80s, congregation secretary Lillian Eschmann at First Trinity, Oakland, Calif., learned to use the computer to prepare the weekly church bulletin. *(William Nettle)*

The Villalobos children of Bellingham, Wash., pile on Dad after he arrives home from fishing. Pictured from front to back are Evan, Candido, Addie, Vance and Kathrine. The family attends Trinity, Bellingham. *(Carl Sahlhoff)*

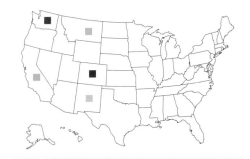

Members of Avondale Church, Woodinville, Wash., enjoy a weekend retreat at Valley Camp, North Bend, Wash. Front, from left: Diana Kimball, Jill Kiehl, Pastor Richard Schmidt, Dana Loechelt, Alice Schmidt. Back row: Denice Peterson, Elsa Schmidt, Dorothy Marwood, Kathy Vincent, Eunice Schmidt, Jennie Bryden. *(Kathy Kiehl)*

The youth of Our Savior, Arcadia, Calif., prepare dinner for the homeless at the Union Station Mission in Pasadena. *(Rick Krach)*

Harry Garguild, member of First Trinity, Oakland, Calif., vacuums the vestry on a monthly cleanup day. *(William Nettle)*

On the Big Island of Hawaii, Phil Zabell, left, pastor of Our Savior, Aiea, Hawaii, asks God to bless the house of Anna and Stuart Barte. Other friends look on. *(James A. Arendale)*

Banner Committee members Martha "Marty" Stewart, left, and Eileen Riske hang the banner for Good Shepherd Sunday at Redeemer, Thousand Oaks, Calif. *(Theodore R. Dibble)*

In the cream of things: After a week of shooting roll upon roll of *smiling, clinging, singing* and *splashing,* photographer Felix Rivera of Bethany, Long Beach, Calif., had to get one more shot—a birthday self-portrait with his family. From left, Inez Gerloff, Alex Rivera, Felix Rivera, Sam Rivera and Elsie Rivera.

It's prom night at Martin Luther High School, Northrop, Minn. Looking their best are, from left, John Mumme, Alicia Lindell, Josh Milow, Anne Quade, Dalin Lappe and Robin Dannhoff. *(Ron Royuk)*

Tom Angus, left, third-level black belt instructor in tae kwon do, takes a move from Adam Eggemeyer, student at the green-belt level, at classes through Jefferson College, Arnold, Mo. Tom is on the staff of the LCMS Foundation in St. Louis. Adam is a member of Immanuel, Waterloo, Ill. *(Karen Eggemeyer)*

Car washes and youth group fund-raisers seem to go together. At Christ, Meridian, Miss., Jo Auera turns the hose on a van in need of cleanup. The youth group is raising funds for a congregation member who was paralyzed in an auto accident. *(Linda Abel)*

Many Missouri Synod members can trace family history to a country church like Immanuel in Soldier Township, Charter Oak, Iowa. Many of these rural congregations continue to serve as the center of a faith community as well as a geographic community. *(Kristin Suhr)*

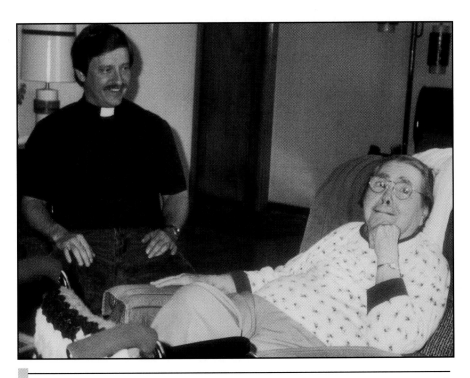

Sharing joy in the Lord, Pastor Curtis Deterding, Faith, Godfrey, Ill., makes a call to homebound member Louise Kuhlmann. *(Carol Kuhlmann)*

Abung Adoku, a Kusasi woman, and her daughter Salamatu display their goat and its kid at a project of the Nasuan Development Centre in Gambaga, Ghana. The Centre is a ministry of LCMS World Relief. *(Linda and Delano Meyer)*

At a community session in Mosio, a small village southeast of Nasuan in Ghana, women discuss changes in the environment. Changes that many noted included reduced crop production, fewer trees, fewer wild animals, less water, a shorter growing season and more illness. *(Linda and Delano Meyer)*

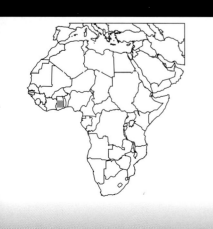

Soil samples in Ghana are very important. These tests showed that the soil needs extra calcium, phosphorous and sulfur, before crops can be grown. The soil-sampling is also a project of the Nasuan Development Centre, Ghana.
(Linda and Delano Meyer)

In the Philippines, Missionary Don Treglown leads his weekly "Pastors Seminar." He is using the Catechism, newly published in Kaulo, and offers tips to his lay preachers on how it can be used as a teaching tool. *(Joanne Treglown)*

The Word of the Lord is spread among the Tagakaulo. From the left, Pablo Bawa; Rufino Grande, Chiquito Angonia (pastor of Quiabol) and Tirso Dulay visiting from Citio Columbio. *(Don Treglown)*

Saturday is Missionary Don Treglown's busiest day; yet he always has time to sit in his hammock and visit with a guest. It's market day in Upper Mainit, and many friends stop by for a chat. *(Joanne Treglown)*

The new day begins a new week, and God's people throughout the lands continue to serve Him and one another. On this Sunday, April 28, 1996, Dr. Dean O. Wenthe, 15th president of Concordia Theological Seminary, Fort Wayne, Ind., welcomes the many worshipers who have come to Kramer Chapel to take part in his installation service. The seminary also is celebrating its 150th anniversary this year, as shown on the banner. *(Gary Penner)*

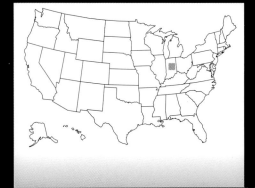

Acknowledgments

The editors of this book express heartfelt thanks to all photographers who participated in this project. We recognize that the selection ultimately becomes subjective, based on quality, content and representation throughout the Synod, and, regrettably, many photos were not published.

Whether your photos were included or not, you photographers *made* this book. Thank you!

Through this project, we have made many friendships by phone, through your notes and letters and the pictures you submitted. We have been touched by your enthusiasm, your love of your Lord and your personal gifts of time and talents for this project.

Editorial and production staff

Managing editor: Roland Lovstad

Coordinating editor: Suzanne Johnson

Photo editor and graphic design: George Ibera

Photo selection: David Faucz, Katie Harrison

Cover design: Tim Agnew

Layout: Ray Jones, Ted Bolte

Production manager: Steve Harris

Production coordinator: Wayne Sell

Production assistants: Ruth Brown, Connie Goodson

Editorial staff: Debb Andrus, Gerry Bode, Julie Doubek, Carla Dubbelde, Karen Eggemeyer, Lois Engfehr, Laine Rosin, Annette Schroeder, John Tape, Jim Wiemers, Rita Wienhoff

Project assistants: Mary Block, Andrea Herrick, Karen Kohlmeyer

Project consultant: Marya McCrae

Product manager: Rick Johnson

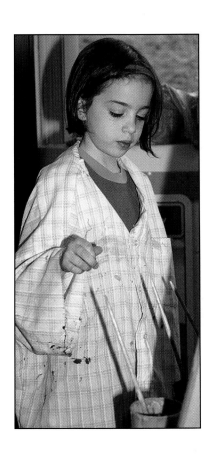

Index of photographers

A

Abel, Linda, 208
Ahlschwede, Dale, 20
Amen, Eugene L., 163
Ames, Richard, 45
Arendale, James A., 75, 77, 131, 157, 207
Arnold, Barbara, 27
Aubry, Art, 46
Auping, Barbara, 34

B

Badertscher, Kathie, 155
Bainbridge, Martha, 15
Barber, Marsha, 14
Barker, Robert L., 32, 57
Barnett, Delinda, 42, 147, 203
Bauer, William, 101
Beechner, Greg, 94, 172
Benke, Judith, 107
Berrey, Bonnie, 38, 93, 121, 144
Beyersdorfer, Dick, 37
Biggs, Mary Lynn, 161
Bird, T., 130
Bisping, Roschelle, 147, 178
Bittner, Paul, 64
Blackwell, Michael, 80
Blackwood, Connie, 19, 140, 141, 163, 193
Bode, Timothy, 73, 148
Boehne, Gary, 124
Brackman, Gene, 24, 98
Brandt, Lani Rose, 74, 97, 150, 179, 204
Bredthauer Jr., Oscar, 176, 201, 202
Brogren, Sherry, 72
Brondos, Charles, 156
Brown, Lisa D., 81, 101, 103
Buerger, Edgar, 186
Buettner, Phyllis M., 51, 74, 102
Buss, Roger G., 112, 195
Buzzell, Thomas, 166

C

Carlson, Roger, 11
Caslow, Timothy J., 56, 161
Cauwet, Raymond, 127

Coit, Kathryn, 41, 43
Cooper, Bill, 60, 81, 117, 170, 196
Cooprider, Jim, 72
CPH, 65, 66, 87, 110

D

Daily, Bea, 16, 82, 189
Davidson, Earl, 99, 131
de la Motte, Mel, 51, 130
Demmin, Dennis, 186
Deverman, Jim, 30, 79
Dibble, Theodore R., 48, 78, 151, 154, 183, 207
Dinger, Nancy, 96
Diller, Gwen, 83
Doenges, Paul W., 192
Droste, Richard, 54, 109
Duncan, David H., 145

E

Edwards, Ardis, 153
Eggemeyer, Karen, 95, 208
Ehlers, Jeff, 100
Essig, Cindy, 72
Etter, Roger, 60

F

Faulkner, Julie, 113, 193, 194
Fearing, James L., 18, 141
Flegler, Brenda, 17, 54, 107, 137, 188
Fuller, LaVern, 46, 69

G

Gabrielson, Jerry, 172
Gamble, John, 180
Garnier, Brian, 187
Garrick, Ken, 43, 203
Gaudette, John, 55, 160
Geisler, Carol, 128, 131
Gill, Dan, 34
Gillenwater, Doris, 109
Gooding, Thelma, 195
Gootee, Doug, 187
Gosney, K.S., 145, 146
Gottschalk, John, 177
Grant, Frank E., 162

Greaney, Andrea M., 56
Greene, Ken, 63, 71, 94, 95, 122, 175

H

Haas, Jane L., 88, 89
Hall, Dennis, 173, 198
Hanes, Toni, 149, 176
Hanke, Herb, 14
Hannum, Garth, 174, 176, 177
Hansen, Fawn, 146
Harff, Lynn, 36
Hassel, John, 21, 59, 113, 134, 139, 165
Hausler, Ray, 32
Hays, Kenneth A., 85
Heckendorf, Bob, Sue, 25, 61
Heller, Phil, 49
Herring, Annette, 35, 40, 67, 198
Hoefle, Lynn, 29, 86, 94, 142
Holm, Marsha L., 106, 190
Holz, Walter L., 191
Honore, Paul, 157
Horst, Carl, 191
Huebner, Peg, 78, 82
Humphries, Doug, 18
Huxsoll, Beverly A., 59, 84, 118, 173, 198, 199

J

Jacob, Roy A., 35, 144, 153
Jensen, Ruta, 27, 88, 142, 195
Johnson, Suzanne, 71, 76, 83, 102, 118, 159, 169, 180
Junas, Lil, 15, 108

K

Kaiser, Marie, 163, 170
Karabinus, Joseph, 57
Kassouf, John, 188
Keinath, Janet, 85
Kettler, Greg, 26, 63, 65
Kiehl, Kathy, 206
Klan, Petr, 114
Knack, Al, 30, 167
Knoche, Jessica, 55, 188
Knuth, Barbara, 70, 193
Krach, Rick, 203, 206
Krahn, Kurt H., 26, 58
Kuehn, Clarice, 70

Kuenzel, Dave, 39, 66, 68, 174, 175
Kuhlmann, Carol, 142, 171, 209

L

Lawrence, Linda, 17, 55, 83, 106, 136, 161
Lee, Steve, 150
Liese, Marc, 137, 171
Lindberg, Gwen, 69, 93, 116, 148, 202
Lindemann, Randy, 28, 29, 62, 116, 166
Loeber, Norman, 47, 98
Loeber, Sally, 73
Lucht, Jane, 167
Lutz, Steve, 132, 133

M

MacDonald, Robert J., 97
Markus, Donald, 179
Materna, Anton, 13
Matson, Mark, 94
Matthys, Tim, 45, 88, 154, 201, 202
Matzke, Gerald, 61, 86
McCune, Christine, 22, 23, 115, 192
McGuire, Judith, 45, 92
McGuire-Klemme, Colleen, 34, 37
Meier, Sheldon, 50
Mennell, Augusta R., 15
Messmann, Greg, 95
Meyer, Linda and Delano, 210
Meyer, Paul, 92
Meyer, Ronald E., 75, 196
Meyer, Vernon, 38
Mickelson, Bob, 24, 129
Miller, Rebecca, 136
Morris, Robert R., 67
Morris, Wendy, 21
Mossner, Eugene D., 160
Mueller, Al, 35, 39
Mueller, Cindy, 115, 197
Mueller, Dawn T., 32
Mueller, Diane L., 117

N

Napora, Patricia Lee, 108
Naumann, Edward, 42, 148
Nelsen, Rick, 25, 29
Nettle, William, 100, 205, 206

Neumann, Howard, 34
Niemann, John M., 18, 58, 59, 87, 119
Nolley Jr., Clarence T., 16

O

Ockrassa, Paul, 40, 90, 91, 156
Ocock, Glenn, 24, 59, 143, 177
Olsen, Peter, 62
Ostermiller, Gary A., 204
Ostrander, Tim, 111, 112
Otto, Marvin D., 144

P

Patton, Jo, 69
Payton, Richard, 121, 190
Penner, Gary, 86, 107, 110, 123, 212
Petzold, Tina, 19
Phillips, Deborah, 20, 110, 127, 192
Pixley, Bonnie, 100, 181
Plvan, George, 171
Polzin, Su, 22
Porter, Eileen, 144
Porter, Shirley, 130, 157
Poulson, Russell H., 140, 141, 194
Proctor, Bill, 201

R

Raasch, Robert A., 200
Rau, Harold M., 68
Redweik, Mildred, 111, 137, 138
Remond, Emelda, 194
Rensvold, Roger F., 43
Repinecz, Gerlinde U., 108
Reuther, Peg, 179
Rick, Fred, 47, 124, 125, 203, 204
Ritz, Elaine, 66
Rivera, Felix, 50, 155, 182
Robinson, Mary H., 21, 85, 110, 112, 175
Roles, John T., 36, 39, 41, 196, 199
Roos, Marlin W., 30, 60, 62, 115, 116
Ross, Barbara, 12, 14, 134, 172, 186
Rowold, Henry, 104
Royuk, Ron, 208
Rummal, William G., 164
Rumsey III, John C., 77, 150, 181

Rychel, Mark, 20

S

Sahlhoff, Carl, 48, 76, 126, 157, 180, 205
Samuels, Bob, 41
Saxton, William, 49
Scattergood, Judy, 181
Schalk, John, 27
Schanke, Karen, 57
Schlobohm, Sara E., 47
Schmidt, Helene E., 138
Schmidt, John, 77, 87, 102, 103, 105, 125, 156,
    182, 183, 205
Schmidt, Yvonne, 106
Schneider, Curt, 28, 61, 168
Schoenfeld, King, 36, 38, 67, 89
Schoepp, Rebecca, 49, 183
Schuller, Addy, 113, 115
Scott, Ann K., 169, 177
Scott, Kathleen, 39, 40, 99, 168, 174, 198
Shiroo, Ken, 173
Sippola, Carol, 57, 84
Smith, Kent, 143
Smith, Larry, 129
Snell, Jerry, 147
Stertz, Nelma, 32, 62
Stewart, Cleone, 35, 37, 40, 66, 118, 121, 197, 200
Strazzante, Scott, 33
Streng, Rosalie, 197
Strobel, Lynda, 42, 149
Stueve, Barry, 74, 76
Suhr, Jennell J., 44
Suhr, Kristin, 145, 209
Swanson, Kent, 54, 135, 191
Swanson, Tom, 17, 88, 120
Switzer, Sue, 70, 178

T

Taylor, Wayne, 49, 152
Thies, Richard N., 43
Thompson, Jane, 127, 151, 155
Tirsell, David, 93, 109, 140
Tonge, David, 26, 53, 58

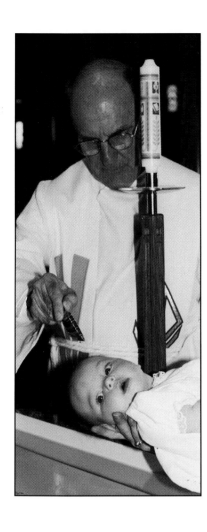

Treglown, Donald, 132, 211
Treglown, Joanne, 211
Truebenbach, Tom, 30
Tufts, Sandie, 151

U

Uyetake, Vern, 84

V

Van Duzer, Thomas N., 44, 96
Voigt, Arnold, 13
Vonderheid, Randy, 178
Voth, Marcus, 80, 81, 135

W

Wagner, Betty J., 148
Wahl, Rhoda, 124, 125, 126
Waldren, Rita A., 187
Walsh, Kristin A., 182
Warner, John, 65, 73, 77, 185
Wegner, Willard G., 128, 135
Weinrich, Philip, 22
Wendland, Walt, 162
Wendorf, Robert B., 143
Wensel, Herman R., 23, 44
Wetters, Ron, 20, 160
White, Ken, 200
Wiese, Ronald, 28, 171
Williams, Roger, 12, 56, 63, 80
Wilson, Lorraine C., 117, 118
Winesburg, Clair, 139, 170
Wing You Tong, 50, 51, 75, 126
Winningham, Dave, 114
Witcraft, Sharon, 92
Witte, Maureen, 78
Wunsch, Kenneth, 15, 189

Y

Yanda, George C., 164
Young, David, 12

Z

Zeller, Ruth, 128

The Lutheran Church—Missouri Synod in its 150th year

6,175 congregations

8,564 pastors

8,822 teachers

281 missionaries (including 126 volunteers, interns and vicars for six months or more)

57 countries where there are mission stations, partner churches or mission relationships

2,601,753 baptized members (1,948,700 communicants)

996 day schools

1,210 early childhood centers (daycare, nursery and preschool)

62 high schools

10 colleges

2 seminaries